THE KINGS OF
SUMMER

Other cricket books by Duncan Hamilton

Harold Larwood: A Biography

A Last English Summer: A Biography

Sweet Summers: The Cricket Writing of J. M. Kilburn

Yorkshire in Wisden (ed)

THE KINGS OF
SUMMER

How Cricket's 2016 County Championship
Came Down to the Very Last Match of the Season

Duncan Hamilton

SAFE HAVEN

First published 2017 by
Safe Haven Books Ltd
12 Chinnocks Wharf
42 Narrow Street
London E14 8DJ
www.safehavenbooks.co.uk

A catalogue record for this book is available from the British Library.

ISBN 978 0 9932911 2 8

10 9 8 7 6 5 4 3 2 1

2021 2020 2019 2018 2017

Typeset in Filosofia and Gill Sans by SX Composing DTP, Rayleigh, Essex
Printed and bound in the UK by Clays Ltd, St Ives plc

For those who love the County Championship

CONTENTS

DAY ONE

Tuesday, 20 September 2017

Middlesex	15	5	0	10	46	37	213
Yorkshire	15	5	2	8	45	39	204
Somerset	15	5	1	9	40	38	203

Attendance: 4,212

Just once I'd like to go to Lord's in the swanky manner of the monocle-wearing C. B. Fry, prodigiously talented as a cricketer-athlete and also prodigiously well off for a while; a gentleman made out of white five-pound notes. Fry's chauffeur would bring his master's Bentley to the red-carpeted entrance of Brown's Hotel and pack the boot with a hamper of chicken sandwiches and hock, a box of Henry Clay cigars, a couple of travelling rugs, a pair of binoculars and a copy of Herodotus' *The Histories*, insurance against a rain-delay or tedium. That is the aristocratic way to get there; but today, the mottled sky carrying the vague threat of a shower or something worse, I am relying as ever on Shanks's Pony to take me to the Grace Gates. I am taking a specific route for a specific purpose; I have a small pilgrimage to make.

It's a minute or so after nine o'clock, and the tail-end of the morning rush hour is travelling along Baker Street more slowly than a state funeral. The air reeks of petrol fumes, but there's a surprising thrum about the low growl of a hundred or so engines, sometimes revved impatiently, and also the occasional, short blast of a horn. It's like listening to a discordant orchestra tuning-up. Double-decker buses heading to Park Lane and Hyde Park Corner, Earls Court and the Fulham Palace Road, lurch forward, their big wheels barely completing two full-turns before halting again. (In this jam Fry's Bentley would get stuck somewhere around Berkeley Square). The traffic is so thick that I'm able to nip and dart among it, noticing the bored exasperation of drivers who would rather be anywhere other than waiting for a light to turn green.

Near the top end of Baker Street, close to the Marylebone Road, I take a sharp turn, walk fewer than 50 yards and find what I'm looking for: a Prussian-blue double-door beneath a stilted arch. Bickenhall Mansions is an example of late Victorian design, craftsmanship and ambition. Warm red brick. Terracotta dressings. High gables. Niches and ornate carvings. Wrought-iron balconies. What it lacks is an English Heritage blue plaque to advertise the fact that the father of modern cricket journalism, which is how John Arlott described him, lived here during the last years of his life. Neville Cardus rented number 112, a one-bedroom basement flat that seemed inappropriately pokey for someone knighted shortly before he moved in. But Cardus found Bickenhall Mansions convenient for Lord's, which is a half-hour amble away.

In the past six months, researching his biography, I've been as zealous in pursuit of Cardus as Boswell was of Johnson. Even the minutiae surrounding him have become important to me. In a way, it's been like living two lives: his and my own. I have re-read his books, his newspaper and magazine articles, and even the scripts of the talks he gave 'on the wireless'. I've gone over his letters. I've watched the television interviews in which he talked in asides and digressions about the Golden Age Trumper and the Silver Age Bradman. In doing so he sounded like a cross between the Ancient Mariner and Old Father Time. He made me wish that the world's physicists would hurry up and invent the Time Machine, enabling us to see what he'd seen.

I got along with Cardus so easily, I suppose, because I share his outsized adoration for the County Championship, the axis on which his every long summer turned. It was desirably everything back then; fit to rank beside an Ashes series, he said. Those who didn't win it envied those who had. During his peak, which came between the wars, the matches pulled in crowds willing to stand 30-deep and more. Newspapers such as his own, the *Manchester Guardian*, devoted long columns of dense type, topped by multi-deck headlines, to them.

Cardus's pieces were the most widely read because he was the first writer to transform a factual report into a sporting literary essay; and also the first to regard a day at the cricket as a piece of theatre. As Cardus saw it, the players were in a play, wrestling with the part given to them. He showed how the everyday is never trivial. Within it he'd nearly always find a sense of occasion, even an epic poem. Cardus was influential to the extent that the way we perceive the history and also the long tradition of the Championship is largely down to the words he left us.

Now what Wordsworth once said of Milton I can say about Cardus: 'Thou shouldst be living at this hour'. No one would relish more the fact that out of the last gasp of this year's Championship comes such a roaring conclusion, a final round of matches that will produce one of three winners. It's as if the rarest conjunction of planets has just rolled into view. At Taunton, Somerset, who are third, face Nottinghamshire, already relegated and in disarray. At Lord's, the centre of the game's great geography, it's Middlesex versus Yorkshire, which also means first versus second. Cardus would demand a box seat. For while blood and birth, as well as professional obligation, welded him to Lancashire, he also identified with — and had a tender heart for — Yorkshire and Yorkshiremen.

And, apart from the Roses match, in which 'fair cheatin' all round' was infamously permissible, a fixture that always fascinated him was Middlesex v Yorkshire – the epitome of top hat versus cloth cap, the north 'tekkin' on the south'.

It's presumptuous to speak for the dead, but I have an inkling that the old boy would find the circumstances surrounding this game supremely ironic. The Championship, badly maligned for most of the season, is speaking up for itself again. He'd add his threepenny-worth to the debate about its future. About the role – even the very survival – of some of the less well-off, less popularly-supported counties. About the place of Twenty20 in the calendar. About the question of whether – and how much – the Championship matters, and what could be lost without it.

Wherever I've gone to watch the Championship this summer, Cardus has come with me in spirit. So it's fitting, today of all days, that I should call on him personally at last. In his mid-eighties he was described as being as 'loose and thin as a puppet', and of walking 'with little high-stepping movements, as though the road was made of burning coals'. His face was gaunt and wizened, his thin hair slicked back and a pair of dark-framed spectacles hung over sticky-out ears. He nearly always wore a pale-grey suit and carried a black umbrella.

A gigantic leap of the imagination isn't needed to picture him emerging from his semi-subterranean existence in Bickenhall Mansions, coming down the five broad steps separating threshold from pavement, and striding towards Lord's at a brisk lick. He'd skirt Dorset Square, where Thomas Lord, dismissed as 'nobbut a market gardener good at growing grass', cut his first pitch. He'd go past the glass canopy of Marylebone Station. He'd walk along Lisson Grove, beyond the spot where Lord cut his second pitch. Finally, he'd cross the St John's Wood Road. I am going this way too; and, after all the time I've spent with him, friendship compels me to start from here. Nowhere else would be at all appropriate.

Mid-to-late September is melancholic, almost mournful for me. Leaves, every hue of rust-brown, are strewn everywhere in Dorset Square, choking up the paths and the kerbsides, a forewarning that the cricket season is about to end. The earth has a damp, peaty smell. Scattered beneath some of the trees along Lisson Grove I come across the odd conker, shiny bright as a new ball. That early nights will soon be here, the clocks pushed back, is inescapable. I try to forget that as I approach Lord's, but there's a pressing need to mine as much as can possibly be got from what's left of 'the summer', which for any cricket-watcher – irrespective of what the meteorologists say – beats on until the last ball is bowled.

Beside the Grace Gates, where a straggly queue has already formed, a man of late middle age is wearing a wide straw hat, a herringbone jacket and a pair of salmon-pink trousers, almost luminous in the murk. He is chuntering on to whoever will listen. His primary audience is someone conspicuously 'Yorkshire' – a White Rose fastened to the lapel of his blazer, a rolled-up copy of the *Yorkshire Post* in his hand. 'Not been as easy for us as we thought,' says the Yorkshireman, without a murmur of an accent from any of the four Ridings. 'Thought we'd stroll it, frankly,' he adds, shaking his head. It's as if still being in contention for the Championship, rather than already possessing it, is insufficient for a county that considers the trophy tantamount to a family heirloom bequeathed to them by Lord Hawke. When you're living in a golden age, I suppose you don't want to settle for brass. Yorkshire began the season as overwhelming favourites, expected to emulate what another Yorkshire team, under the captaincy of the indomitable Brian Close, achieved 48 years before – a hat-trick of Championships. Seven counties have tried and failed to match the feat since. Middlesex are one of them; Durham, Essex, Surrey, Sussex, Warwickshire and Worcestershire are the others: a roll call of gallant failure emphasising the difficulty of the task.

The match has an added poignancy for Yorkshire. It marks Jason Gillespie's farewell as coach, his return to Australia telegraphed through a grapevine buzz of rumours long before formal confirmation came three weeks ago. Anyone not born in Yorkshire usually doesn't qualify for the county's passport status for half a century at least; and even then straightforward longevity of residence is no guarantee of acceptance. Gillespie warrants preferential treatment, his anointment as an honorary Yorkshireman given for outstanding achievement.

In a marriage every fight tends to be the same fight, over and again, in slightly different disguises. Too often Yorkshire's cricket has seemed a bit like that too. In his play, *A Day Out*, Alan Bennett, takes his characters, who are members of a cycling club, to Fountains Abbey, where there's a picnic and a cricket match. One of the Abbey's 12th-century inner walls becomes the wicket, drawn on shakily with a stub of chalk. The outfield is a grassy oblong from which clumps of wild flowers spout. Someone produces a bat, the wood as dark as anthracite and wrapped thickly with twine. Someone else produces a ball without a seam. What begins as a competitive but friendly contest dissolves into a finger-pointing argument about pride, ego and entitlement. Afterwards, nearly everyone goes off in a huff. It's as though Bennett is portraying in microcosm Yorkshire's disputatious history. But by being a unifying presence, practical and phlegmatic, Gillespie has rid his Yorkshire of that sort of reputation. He's made the team into a cumulative power. In his first season he got promotion from Division Two. In his second, Yorkshire were First Division runners-up. Then came those back-to-back titles. The odds, it has to be said, are against a third Championship for him.

As the table stands, Yorkshire must beat Middlesex and gain maximum bonus points. Somerset's hope of leapfrogging both of them hinges on one of two scenarios. The first, thumping Notts out of sight, is almost certain to happen. Somerset will prepare what's become commonly known as a 'Ciderbad' pitch bespoke for their spinners: Jack Leach, who has claimed 58 wickets, and the lean, 19-year-old Dom Bess, whose debut against Warwickshire at the start of the month brought him 6 for 28 and then 2 for 31. The second scenario – that Middlesex and Yorkshire will labour over a draw – is unlikely. Even if the weather turns rotten, pushing a result at Lord's into one of those unreachable places, there could be a contrived finish that would nullify, however cruelly, even Somerset's best efforts.

A contrived finish could be needed anyway. Middlesex have only twice been successful at home: once at Merchant Taylors' School, one of those small arenas of the Championship so integral to the competition's enduring appeal, and once at Lord's against lowly Durham. That match was Middlesex's first win there since last September when Yorkshire took the title – scrambled runs securing the necessary bonus points – and then lost the match so implausibly that you checked and re-checked the scoreboard next morning to be sure someone wasn't mischievously pulling your leg. Middlesex made a decent fist of that summer, finishing as runners-up but a whopping 68 points adrift. The sight of Yorkshire parading the gold chalice at Lord's, like some conquering army that's just captured the castle, proved a red-rag moment for Middlesex, galvanising them for this season.

A week ago I went to Old Trafford to watch them against a struggling Lancashire, a game which ought to have made this one irrelevant. At one stage, replying to Middlesex's respectable 325, Lancashire were in deep water at 6 for 4. One more shove would have drowned them. Middlesex lacked the ruthlessness to do it. From a seat so high in a stand that Manchester's cityscape, swathed in a haze of heat, rolled into the far distance, I saw below the 20-year-old makeshift opener, Rob Jones, drive and cut his way into Lancashire's record books. After every boundary he struck, Jones walked to the non-striker's end, tapping his bat into it superstitiously, as though some curse would come upon him if he didn't. He held off Middlesex for six hours and 45 minutes and carried his bat, the youngest to do so in the Championship for Lancashire since Cyril Washbrook in 1935. Jones even brought up his century audaciously: three steps down the pitch and a steepling six over long-on. Against his dogged resistance, Middlesex offered . . . well, not much, actually. Their chins too often touched their chests. Their bowlers lost their line. Their fielding deteriorated. The match, theirs to be grasped, petered out into a draw.

Across the Pennines, Yorkshire fared even worse at Headingley, embarrassingly suffering a ten-wicket defeat to Somerset after being bustled out in the first innings for a measly 145. Even a second-innings century from Jake Lehmann only delayed the inevitability of defeat.

That result was responsible for triangulating the race. So we've all packed our radio, our phone, our iPad – anything that allows us, electronically at least, to be simultaneously in two places at once. Taunton, though 143 miles distant, will seem like next door, what happens there shaping what happens here.

At the beginning of his career Neville Cardus, rawly callow and insecure, disliked Lord's. The frosty protocols there – 'The place is a mass of signboards, teaching you your manners and position in life,' he complained – and the snootiness of high falutin' members appalled him. He trod warily, afraid of being rebuked for errors of etiquette, the rules of which were unknown to him, or for not bowing at the correct angle.

Oh, dear. I know how he feels. As soon as I get inside the ground there is some fussy, know-your-place palaver. In less than five minutes I'm told four times where I can't sit or stand, and in which direction I'm not allowed to walk. I want a far-off peek at the pitch on my way to the upper tier of the Compton Stand. I glimpse it in the gap between the Allen Stand and the pavilion before I'm barked at. The steward doing the barking is concerned that a toe of mine might trespass on to the turf, which apparently will cause some cataclysmic cosmic disturbance. His ire seems misplaced, because the outfield is a chaotic swarm of people, most of them either television technicians or Lord's officials, rushing about with folders and clipboards, their eyes often turned towards the clouds, which are slowly darkening.

A friend of mine wonders why going to a County Championship cricket match should not be like going to a National Trust property. Non-members would then be greeted as a guest rather than a mere spectator. You would be genuinely welcomed, in a pleased-to-see-you and come-back-soon sort of way. And at the end of your day, you'd feel that becoming a member would not only be worthwhile, but also imperative, so politely have you been treated by this civilised institution: a part of things rather than apart from them.

But far too frequently, and particularly at Lord's, the impression persists that the paying customer is a bit of a pest; he can be treated grumpily, and even barely toler-ated, because he's sure to come back anyway. The game may want to re-think that attitude before the real pests among us decide otherwise. When eventually I reach the Compton Stand, the scoreboard sends out a greeting: WELCOME TO LORD'S. YOUR HOME OF CRICKET. It strikes me as someone's idea of black humour.

Looked down on, rather than flatly across, the pitch is a little greener than I imagined it would be. The ground staff are tidying up the whole square. Dust is being swept. Grass is being cut, the faintest scent of it blowing this way. Tired patches worn to bare soil are stomped carefully even.

With an hour until play begins, I wander towards the Nursery End nets. The nets allow the amateur brief intimacy with the professional. You can get close enough to hear the fizz of spin in flight, the hard *tock* of ball off bat and the scrape of studs, a slipped curse, the swishing sound a fast delivery makes when it bulges against the back of the netting. You're on top of everything like a close-in fielder. Cardus, coming to Lord's for the first time, stood behind Jack Hobbs' net, mesmerised by the Master's footwork. It was as though Hobbs was tap-dancing with a bat in his hand. I watch the Middlesex opener Nick Gubbins, who has already scored almost 1,200 runs this season, and the pacy Toby Roland-Jones, summoned but not used by England in mid-summer.

Roland-Jones isn't over-exerting himself. He's gently limbering up, bending his back and stretching his shoulders. Sometimes he stops, looks distractedly around him and scratches his chin, pulling at his thin black beard in concentrated thought. And sometimes he takes a practice ball, throwing it up and catching it again without looking. You half-expect he'll suddenly produce two more from his pocket and start juggling. When he does bowl, his speed is well below half pace.

Gubbins, dressed in Middlesex's navy training kit, pummels balls repeatedly into the net, an exercise designed to improve hand speed. Satisfied that he's done enough, he wipes the sweat of the practice shift off his brow and tucks his bat under his arm. On the long walk to the dressing room he passes a gaggle of early arrivals. He's out of earshot when one of them asks: 'Who's that?' No one knows, which says something depressing about the Championship's profile.

In the cigarette-card age the yeoman cricketer went virtually unrecognised except in his own backyard. The image on those cards wasn't big or clear enough to make his face instantly familiar. Television, significantly the arrival of the John Player League on the BBC in 1969, made a difference, allowing you to identify everyone if you were interested enough. Now domestic cricket isn't shown on a terrestrial channel; there's barely a flicker of it even on the news. And the grille of the helmet is like the Lone Ranger's mask, guaranteeing the face a level of anonymity.

But Gubbins won't be inconspicuous for much longer, I suppose. He's meant for a higher peak. What's more, he can confirm it soon enough; Yorkshire have decided to bowl. Nothing abides but change, and the County Championship offers regular proof of that. No season, alas, is organisationally a mirror-image of the last. What the ECB regards as experimental innovation, which is no more than management-speak euphemism, often seems like mucking about for the sake of it. Or for reasons of expediency. Or because of befuddled, spongy thinking. Every winter we wait for the tinkering. Every summer we come to terms with it.

The newest tweak, modernity trampling again over tradition, is the uncontested toss, which allows the visiting captain the choice of bowling first. What I liked was the ceremony, the mini-pageant of going to the middle, which you could observe through binoculars. Ever since Yorkshire's sestercentennial anniversary in 2013, the captain has always put on his blazer, pin-striped yellow and pale blue in homage to the original tailoring of Lord Hawke's. It added a nice formality to something time-honoured. I miss the flip of the coin and always, from expression and hand-gesture, being able to guess who had called correctly before the tannoy announced it.

It's become gloomier in the past half-hour. There's a sticky dampness in the air and the clouds have collided, sinking so low that I begin to fret about the light. No need. On time first Yorkshire and then Nick Gubbins and his partner Sam Robson clip down the stone steps and through the pavilion gate. Gubbins continually rehearses his forward defensive stroke, signalling how obdurate Middlesex intend to be.

From the pavilion end Ryan Sidebottom takes 16 paces and rakes a boot across the grass before stomping his white disc into it. Sidebottom missed more than three months of the season after treading on a football instead of kicking it, fracturing his ankle. Yesterday he signed a new one-year contract for Yorkshire. Today, at 38, he is hunting for the sixth Championship of his career. He *is* one of the county cricketers who everyone knows on sight; not only because he's made 22 Test appearances, but also because of his mop of curly brown hair. With the addition of a snug Van Dyck collar, and a big hat with a feather in it, he'd fit unobtrusively into the court of Charles I.

There's a crowd of 1,500 here for the start, well spread between the Compton and Edrich stands, the Mound Stand, the Tavern Stand and the pavilion. The Grandstand is closed, as empty as a beach in January, because work to rebuild the Warner Stand beside it is on-going more than 12 months after demolition began. As Sidebottom whirls his left arm repeatedly, like a windmill caught in a gale, a few latecomers dive urgently in, afraid of missing the opening over and doubtlessly aware of what doing so meant a year ago.

In the first over of this match last September, again from the Compton Stand, I witnessed Sidebottom's triple-wicket maiden. I also witnessed the incredulity of those who unfortunately arrived too late to see it. They looked from the scoreboard to the pitch, and then back again, at the evidence: Middlesex 0 for 3. One man pressed his hands to the side of his face in inconsolable horror, his mouth a black oval, his eyes wide and popping. In that moment, whether he knew it or not, he became Munch's *The Scream*.

This time, as Sidebottom takes an initial, bouncing step before slipping into the steady rhythm of his run, he does so to a solemn hush. The only noise is the clink and din of a hammer and the drone of a drill from the construction of the Warner Stand.

Robson gets through the over, but looks sluggish doing so, like someone battling his limitations. His feet disobey when his mind tells them where to go. There is a narrow squeak for him. Without much conviction, he decides to leave the fifth ball, which whooshes past the off stump so closely that the back-draught could have blown away a bail. From the outset Gubbins is a sturdier proposition. The maker's logo – he uses a Kookaburra bat – is on full display, like a piece of product-placing. Whereas Robson looks somewhat tucked up and cramped, Gubbins, who is 6 foot tall, stands straight, his wrists cocked and the bat held above the level of the stumps. He plays straight, too, his initial ambition seldom beyond the coaching-manual V.

Gubbins' poster hero is Andrew Strauss, understandable since he's another left-hander, another ex-Middlesex opener and another Old Radleian. There's something of Strauss in the way in which he accumulates his scores, winnowing his range of shots until he's built a robust platform – 35 is Gubbins' benchmark – and becomes more expansive. He picks up the length early, and the positive stride he takes towards the ball or back into the crease is indicative of someone brimming with the self-belief that runs bring. You study Gubbins and then study Robson, realising in the comparison how vital the infinitesimal – the spilt-second

– is in batting. Gubbins waits, letting a delivery come to him, a matter of concentration and self-restraint. Robson gropes, which throws him off balance.

Sidebottom's new ball partner is Jack Brooks, as ever wearing a wide headband that makes him look bandit-like. It's as if he's been charged up with an electric current, immediately giving Middlesex the bonus of four byes with a wild ball that evades wicketkeeper Andy Hodd's dive. Brooks' is a muscular action. His shoulders and his back heave into the final stride, and he can make the hard ball spit wickedly. The harassed-looking Robson finds this out. Not off the mark, he's pecked tentatively at 14 deliveries. To the 15th, his footwork is awry. He moves back and across, tangling himself up in an awkward half-stumble. His weight is in the wrong place. He falls, ungainly, into the ball, which smacks against his pads. The roar of Brooks' appeal is loud enough to be heard in the Lock and Laker Stand at the Oval. Middlesex are 11 for one.

It's the ideal start for Yorkshire, who have had to overcome a fractious build-up to the game. Since the spotlight's arc has shifted for once from Twenty20, giving the Championship the chance to promote itself, you'd have thought the ECB would want a showpiece affair with balloons and bunting. Instead, it intransigently refused to release Jonny Bairstow – despite Bairstow's passionate desire to play for Yorkshire– so as not to weary him for the forthcoming winter tours. This is odd. Five days of cricket is all Bairstow has played in five weeks. It is odder still because no block was placed on Middlesex's Steven Finn, accompanying Bairstow to Bangladesh next month.

Yorkshire are used to juggling resources to cope with international demands. At Trent Bridge, during the one-day series against Sri Lanka, it was practically a Yorkshire and the Rest of England XI against the tourists. In the team were Bairstow, Joe Root and the all-rounders David Willey, Adil Rashid and Liam Plunkett, who smashed a winning, last-ball six 'into the confectionary stand and out again'.

But as well as Bairstow and Root – the latter too pre-cious a jewel to face Middlesex even in these circumstances – Yorkshire are missing two other players: Jake Lehmann, recalled by South Australia, and wrist-spinner Rashid, his absence more incomprehensible than Bairstow's. Rashid pulled out, originally citing a personal issue – a family illness – and then also his mental and physical state, fragile after a 'heavy period' of games. Yorkshire's captain, Andrew Gale, was deliberately terse in response: "I'll take 11 lads on to the field who will give everything to win', he said. The club's supporters, gathered in companionable knots around Lord's, are transparently behind him and 'agin' Rashid. 'Does the lad know,' asks one of them, 'that Wilfred Rhodes used to bowl a thousand overs *every* season?'

Judging from the early scuffles, Yorkshire may not need Rashid. Nick Compton isn't much more impressive than Robson. A nervy edge, racing past third slip, gets him off the mark. There is the crispness of an on-driven four to admire later on, but his innings is mostly prods and indecision, until Brooks jams him in front of the stumps too. The ball comes up the hill and is nearly on top of Compton before he unaccountably shoulders arms. It grazes the roll. Momentarily Compton stands immobile. Then he walks a pace or two across his crease, as if about to demand a referral in super-slow-motion, before trudging away, leaving Middlesex on 33 for 2.

In the rigorous warm-up, carried out in front of the Grandstand, I'd watched Jason Gillespie steering thrown balls off the thick edge or the full blade of the bat towards the cupped hands of Gale and Adam Lyth, Azeem Rafiq and Tim Bresnan. Barely anything was grassed, let alone fumbled. As dress rehearsals go, it couldn't have been slicker. When the catching is for real, however, Yorkshire's fingers are buttered. Two chances go down before lunch. The first, at second slip, isn't too costly. Going to his right, chasing a nick from Dawid Malan at ankle height, Lyth spills it, the ball ricocheting off the hard, fleshy part of his hand below the thumb. Malan, on 19, makes only another three before Willey tempts him into a waft that deflects the ball on to the off stump, reducing Middlesex to 57 for 3. It's revenge for Willey, belted for 15 from a messy opening over.

The second mistake, at backward point, could be a capstone event. In the Compton Stand there'd been some surprise – and this is putting it mildly – that Yorkshire preferred Steve Patterson ahead of Liam Plunkett. Patterson is reliably metronomic, each big-booted step to the wicket identical to the last. He sheds a lot of sweat in being economical, but Plunkett is more explosive, which makes him more likely to stir the batsmen up. Patterson always makes it difficult for them to score. Plunkett always makes it difficult for them to survive.

Patterson does nonetheless trouble Gubbins. Loping in from the pavilion end, he drops a ball a fraction wide and a smidgeon short. Gubbins rocks lightly back on his heels, attempting to slash it square. The delivery isn't as juicy as he thinks it is. The ball climbs on him and the contact he makes isn't clean. The shot slides off the bottom of the bat. Nine times out of ten Rafiq would seize the chance without fuss. He sees it well and early enough, lifting his hands above his right shoulder and correctly calculating trajectory, but not propulsion. His hold on the ball is brief. The chance goes in and immediately squirts out again, soaring upwards. The ball travels above and then behind him, as if it has some squirming life of its own. Rafiq half-pirouettes in pursuit. His head is up. His arms are outstretched. His eyes follow the spinning flight. But he's also aware that gravity is going to beat him unless he makes the sort of long dive that will filthy the knees of his flannels. He sprawls forward, hitting the turf with a bump and rolling into an undignified heap. The ball drops a foot and a half away from him.

If Gubbins' stomach has just done a somersault, he doesn't betray it. He turns the bat in his hand and nonchalantly looks around him. The best batsmen never play the last ball when the next one is coming at them. Gubbins, it seems, possesses that unflappability. Neither this close shave nor two others – a fair shout for lbw and an edge that nearly carries to the slips – bother him. You get the feeling there could be a small detonation at square leg, but Gubbins would simply saunter down the pitch, wipe away an imaginary speck of dirt and settle back into his stance. His maiden Championship century came against Surrey in May. The spectacular follow-up was an unbeaten 201 against Lancashire. Today he's staking out his territory with judicious defence and a smattering of delicious strokes: a cover drive off Brooks is all power; a lean-back dab off Wiley is all finesse; a firm clip off his legs through mid-wicket off Patterson is the epitome of impeccable timing.

At lunch Gubbins has scored exactly half of Middlesex's 84 for 3. Somerset, we discover, have gone from an uncertain 33 for 2 to 99 without further loss, thanks to their captain, Chris Rogers, and James Hildreth, who is batting with a runner and hobbling like a peg-leg pirate after Notts' Jake Ball struck him flush on the right ankle with a yorker.

In this long-distance race no team is shaking off the other two. Yet.

■ ■ ■

It isn't quite on the same scale as the queue of those horse-drawn carriages that would trundle in from the city and line the St John Wood's Road, unloading eager passengers once word spread that WG was batting. All the same, as the afternoon begins, Lord's is filling up.

I like to watch this from the Compton Stand not only because of the view, but also in deference to the eponymous hero. In old action photographs snapped during the 1940s and early 1950s, a lithe Denis Compton in his pomp is seen in the dash of mid-stroke, a lank or two of hair escaping from his otherwise immaculately Brylcreemed short back and sides.

But I recall the man who, during my infant days in journalism, would half-waddle into the Press Box wearing a V-neck sweater bulging against his Falstaffian belly. His once coal-black hair was white-grey and a touch unruly. He'd smile with a genuine solicitude, as though I were really a somebody rather than everyone's gopher, and then politely ask for a telephone. This was ostensibly to speak to the *Sunday Express*, for whom he was a long-time columnist. In reality he was ringing his bookmaker. He'd offer an equally polite 'Thank you' after I found a phone for him, and another at the end of the call.

What I recall, too, is the way the men who had been boys when he was the most glamorous name in cricket would look at him with awe, almost genuflecting. Compton was still wowing them a quarter of a century after his retirement, proving his ever-lasting stardom.

Yorkshire's crowds, unshowy roundheads, thought he was too insouciantly cavalier as a player. His sponsorship deal with Brylcreem was considered to be a touch fancy-dan for those content to slick a dab of lard through their hair on a Saturday night. Once at Sheffield's Bramall Lane, after a dog escaped onto the outfield, Compton gave chase and caught it. He carried the mongrel to the pavilion gate, where it bit him on the forearm. He dropped the animal and began rubbing the welt. An unsympathetic voice growled: 'Put some bloody Brylcreem on it, Compton'.

Today's raucous choir lack such sandpapery wit. There are random choruses of 'Coom on Yorksheer,' the pronunciation of each word monotonously elongated. As much as anything, it's a way of keeping their spirits up. For this session, like most of the first, soon belongs to Nick Gubbins, which brings more rueful reflection about Azeem Rafiq's dropped catch. At lunch Gubbins received his county cap in front of the pavilion, a potentially risky piece of scheduling because the flummery – the handshakes, the photographs, the backslapping – could so easily have skewed his focus. But, far from being disruptive, the presentation propels him on, his purpose renewed.

Since Gubbins can't monopolise the strike, a route into the Middlesex tail opens up for Yorkshire nevertheless. Steve Eskinazi, trapped on the crease, jabs a delivery on to his stumps from Jack Brooks. He's made only 12. With the firmest resolution, John Simpson, a fine foil for Gubbins, hangs around for 76 balls before Tim Bresnan, pelting in from the pavilion end, bamboozles him. The delivery that instinct tells Simpson will go harmlessly wide instead zags back. He's lbw for 15, his bat askew across his body. At 154 for five, Yorkshire think themselves on the cusp of a major push. Gubbins, gluing together the middle order, disabuses them of the notion. Yorkshire repeatedly find hope snatched away from them.

Gubbins is never hasty – his 50 comes up in 92 balls – but he isn't tentative either when anything loose appears in front of him. There's one luxurious drive off Jack Brooks. Another, equalling it, dispatches David Willey, who frowns and marches away. A third stroke, the most accomplished, pings a drifting leg-side ball from Steve Patterson wide of midwicket, the harmonious movement and execution behind it seemingly effortless.

Against Gubbins, or anyone else, Yorkshire haven't bowled badly; Bresnan has even found some reverse swing. What has sorely let them down – and does so again – is the fielding. Under the heading *Coaching Tips* in *The Cricketers' Who's Who*, Middlesex's captain James Franklin suggests a batsman shouldn't 'fear' the lofted shot because there are 'a lot of gaps *above* the fieldsmen'. He now discovers there are gaps *through* them too. Franklin is settling in, his eyes barely accustomed to the dimness of the afternoon, when he edges Bresnan to second slip. The catch zips to Gary Ballance at lower-rib height, the task to take it routine. The ball passes through the hands. Franklin is as flabbergasted as the rest of us. It's as if the Ballance in front of us is a hologram, his physical self somewhere else. There's a groan from Yorkshire's faithful, and the predictable 'Coom on Yorksheer' is full of withering disapproval.

Injustice follows that despair; for even when Yorkshire finally take a catch, the umpire neither hears the touch, thin as a cat's whisker, nor registers the minimal deflection it causes. Nick Gubbins went into tea on 96 not out. He's still that one good blow away from his hundred when Ryan Sidebottom comes in from the pavilion end, letting go of a stock ball, slightly mis-aimed. It whips across Gubbins with no wicked speed, no appreciable wobble. Gubbins' strength has been his assessment of line.

Whether through weariness or nerves, so close to his fourth Championship century, he finally errs, nudging casually as he aims to score behind square. Andy Hodd gathers the ball a yard outside leg stump and celebrates like a lottery winner. He chucks the thing skyward, awaiting confirmation of what he knows, absolutely and irrefutably, is Gubbins' goodbye. The slips join in. Gubbins doesn't twitch or budge. The umpire Rob Bailey has his hands clasped in front of him like someone about to pray. He shakes his head. He mouths 'No' twice. Convinced about the guilty edge, and convinced also that Gubbins is aware of it, Yorkshire are dumbfounded and angry. At the over's end Sidebottom walks into the deep with the pain of the wronged man.

Gubbins does more than bat on, his imperturbability a kind of mental armour plating. When Sidebottom returns, seeking vengeance, Gubbins fastens onto a delivery pitched outside off stump that is only a foot short. With a strong-arm pull, he clears not only four leg-side fielders but also the boundary. The ball rattles into the Grandstand seats for six. Off comes the helmet. Up goes the bat. Out go the arms, embracing the applause for his century. It took some muscle – and a lot of brass neck – to play the shot at all.

To the naked eye the day is brighter than it has been for hours. Certainly it seems more conducive to play now than it was first thing this morning. So at 4.55 p.m. there's a collective gasp, and then considerable jeering and moaning, when the teams go off for bad light. Middlesex are 208 for five. The shine on the new ball, which Yorkshire took recently, looks as though someone has wax-polished it.

What follows is an avoidable pantomime. The umpires shuttle between the pavilion and the square, checking and re-checking the light. Tim Robinson, the other umpire, is interviewed in the middle by Sky, which means anyone watching from an armchair knows more about what's going on than the paying customer. We wander around, waiting for the scoreboard or the tannoy, or indeed *anyone*, to tell us why the floodlights aren't being powered up. Perhaps someone is scuttling around in search of a shilling to feed the meter. The lights from both dressing rooms are switched on, glaring at us from either end of the pavilion like a pair of gleaming eyes. The scoreboard is on full beam too, again flashing up the stock phrase WELCOME TO LORD'S. It's as if someone thinks constant repetition of those words will be a comfort. At last, taking pity on us, one steward asks another steward, who finds out from a third that Westminster Council allows Lord's to use to the floodlights only 14 times per season. This season's quota is already spent.

Somerset have crumbled to 322 for 9, tarnishing what went before. The two centurions, James Hildreth and Chris Rogers, put on 269, but seven wickets fell for 20 in 22 balls – five of them for nought. Hildreth is the hero, making 135 while using his bat as a walking stick. On Twitter there's a photograph of his damaged ankle, the spreading bruise every dark colour you can imagine. It's as if someone has whacked him with a blacksmith's hammer. Somerset have three bonus points to Middlesex's and Yorkshire's one apiece, a consolation of sorts for them.

It's time to depart, because it's pointless to stay. The decision is made just as the belated announcement that 'No further play will be possible' reaches us.

WELCOME TO LORD'S, the scoreboard says again.

DAY TWO

Wednesday 22 September 2017

Middlesex	15	5	0	10	47	37	214
Somerset	15	5	1	9	43	38	206
Yorkshire	15	5	2	8	45	40	205

Attendance: 5,258

At the beginning of the season, on a cold, murky mid-April morning, I caught the train from Leeds to Burley Park and took the slightly rising, zig-zag route from there to Headingley to watch Yorkshire against Hampshire. Even on such a short excursion – you can complete the journey in less time than it takes to bowl an over – I picked out immediately those passengers who were going to the cricket with me. For one thing, we were all well insulated, prepared for the great outdoors with padded jackets and sweaters, scarves and tweed flat caps.

For another, we carried the kind of tattered baggage that had seen a lot of match-day service. The bags rattled with flasks and snappin' boxes of sandwiches. For a third, we either thumbed *Playfair*, the spine of the pocket paperback then shiny and relatively uncreased, or pored over the match reports of the previous day's play in the newspapers.

We were there because this was the Championship, and we needed our fix of it after the long, empty winter. We, the Championship's hardcore supporters, are enraptured romantics, as different from the casual observer as the traveller is from the tourist. Even the most sullen weather forecast doesn't put us off.

Headingley was as un-Spring-like as it could possibly be. The cold had teeth in it. The sky was lowering, like an awning, and soon the floodlights were burning through the gloom. You sought whatever shelter you could find. I went on to the back row of the top deck of the ramshackle football stand, a wooden structure that inspires no sonnets and sometimes can be heard creaking. No one anticipated much out of the match. We certainly weren't expecting what we got: an opening session that became a meteor shower of shot-making. Here are the relevant statistics. Hard though it is to believe, none of what follows contains a misprint. Jonny Bairstow, unbeaten on 107 overnight, claimed a double hundred. Liam Plunkett came in at 11.52 a.m. At 1 p.m. he was 94 not out (his century took only 74 minutes and 82 balls). Against a depleted attack, he and Bairstow thrashed and bashed everything everywhere – an amalgam of textbook strokes and improvisation imported from Twenty20, a kind cricketing jazz. The *Guardian* summed it up best of all. The scoreboard revolved, it said, 'like a fruit machine'. Before lunch Yorkshire scored 236 runs in 31 overs. As brutally brilliant as Bairstow was, Plunkett's hitting was more spectacular. One of his 18 fours – there were also two sixes – came close to decapitating his partner. The shot, dragged from off to on, would have stunned a whale. Bairstow, his life flashing before him, ducked at the last second.

Following the Championship is undoubtedly a passion and, for some, unquestionably a vocation. Those who don't like it, dismissing the four-day game as a tour de force of wasting time, often ask me why I love it. Let me count the ways, I reply. I love the quiet, ruminative atmosphere. I love the small, comfortable rituals of match-day: buying a scorecard, even though the modern scoreboards make it unnecessary; the first cup of tea and then the second; a slice of afternoon coffee cake, perhaps; a rummage through the second-hand bookstall. I love the fact you're free to roam around a ground as much as the sun does, watching from wherever the mood takes you – a few overs from directly behind the bowler's arm, a few more parked at deep mid-on or deep square leg or from the highest vantage point you can find, where the set of the field is clearer.

I love another fact: that I can dip in and out of a match as it suits me, missing a day or part of day but catching up with the thread of it again as simply as picking up a put-down book. I also love the soft beat of the game, and the minor but mercurial variations within it; even those slow-slow movements when nothing appears to be happening but, actually, everything sometimes is, such are the nuances of its tactics.

I love its imperfections. Rather like life itself, you endure meandering stretches that appear to have little purpose; periods that are no more inspiring than waiting for a bus. I just let them pass because I love, above all, the camaraderie of Championship cricket. You can watch in solitude while knowing talk and cordial company is easily found if you want it. In his book, *The Game of Life*, Scyld Berry evokes this in a plain but perspicuous sentence of perfect understanding. 'At any county cricket ground,' he says, 'anyone can go and sit beside a stranger and talk without a formal introduction'.

The Championship encourages conviviality. Friend-ships are forged on the basis of like-mindedness and shared experience. The crowd at Headingley, marvelling at Bairstow's and Plunkett's plundering of the bowling, were conscious of that. At lunch, recognising the scarcity of the achievement, everyone began talking to everyone else: analysing it, choosing a favourite shot, even sympa-thising with Hampshire. Pleasure was entwined, too, with a sense of privilege. We congratulated ourselves, crowing aloud to strangers about how astute we'd been to come. How others would envy us. How such prolific run-scoring showed that the Championship wasn't moribund.

It was then – glancing around me – that a disconcerting thought surfaced. Blocks of empty seating are a familiar sight at county games. Yorkshire doesn't open the Western Terrace, which is a pity because the only picturesque view on the ground is found there: the dark, sooty-coloured spire of St Michael's and All Angel's church. But I began to think about the seats that were occupied. Specifically, I considered the people in them. The attendance was around 1,200. Some were in the early bloom or late stages of middle age. Most were older – and a great deal of them were far older, a troubling demographic. These were the long-retired, the kind of men (there were scarcely any women) who metaphorically at least wore their trousers rolled. Their fathers had watched the fag-end of Wilfred Rhodes's career and the beginning of Hedley Verity's. Their father's fathers had watched Major Booth and F. S. Jackson. When cricket first came into their lives, the classical standing of the Championship was unarguable.

But where is the generation to follow my own?

Every lament for a vanished past always sounds like something heard before. The game is never as it once was, of course, and as long ago as 1971 John Arlott thought that it 'may be true' that 'English cricket as we

35

know it is dying'. It wasn't so then, but may be so now. The counties are living in the hardest of hard times, counting halfpennies, and debts that were once inconveniences are looming calamities. Durham have already received a bail-out, counted in millions, which highlighted the absurdity of having too many Test grounds for too few Tests. The ECB has also handed each county £300,000 to 'facilitate cash flow' (the counties ought to press for a greater share of income in the first place rather than relying on extra subsidies).

Outsiders must look at cricket with a cold puzzlement, wondering whether Mr Micawber was once the game's financial adviser but forgot his own definition of happiness and misery. Without a 'proper' Championship, English cricket would be a body without a soul; but I'm afraid this could conceivably happen in a dozen years or so.

At Lord's, I go looking for *any* sign that my view is too pessimistic.

A week ago, sweltering in unexpected heat, it felt more like early July than mid-September. The sun burnt the skin. Yesterday the downward tilt into autumn seemed to have started. Today it is radiant again. There is barely a breath of wind. In a sky of iridescent blue sit only a few torn rags of cloud. The light is strong and ravishingly bright, the kind Turner liked to capture with buckets of yellow paint. Lord's is displaying its plumage; almost every corner of it is a spot of outstanding beauty.

There are hangovers from the previous evening. As the umpires come out, a voice behind me, unmistakably a Yorkshireman's, shouts, 'The light's a bit iffy. Tek 'em off'. There's some chelp and chunter, too, about Nick Gubbins and the feathery leg-side edge that Rob Bailey missed. Though technology isn't being used, Sky does have Snicko. The incriminating spike it registered, trembling like something low on the Richter Scale, was replayed time and again overnight.

Near the red-bricked Print Shop, where you can buy an updated scorecard, I eavesdrop on a three-cornered conversation in which two men fervently believe Gubbins guilty of violating cricket's Corinthian ideals – as if such a spirit was once not only universal but also sacrosanct – and a third is more hard-nosed and practical. 'Walkin'? You can't expect anyone to do it nowadays. It's the umpire's job to give a batsman out,' he says sternly. His accomplices mutter a bit, dredging up 'the halcyon' amateur era, as though everything since has gone to the dogs, before offering only a spluttering, wishy-washy reply to his blunt question: 'Do you *honestly* think that *Sir* Geoffrey Boycott would have walked *for that*?' The words are almost spat out.

The rest is silence until, after a pause more full stop than semi-colon, rubbing the point in becomes irresistible. Bill Lawry, the Australian captain, he reminds them, once trod on his wicket and 'still refused to bloody walk', the umpires giving him the benefit of the doubt. 'Eh,' he adds, tapping his brow: 'you pair are soft in t' head'.

The opening hour and a half is going to be critical. With the ball still new, with the bowlers fresh, Yorkshire have 28 overs to eke out full bowling points. From the start, last night's premature close appears to have worked appreciably for, rather than against, them. There's a crackling energy about the Champions, which was missing yesterday. That was partly because Nick Gubbins, playing a marvellously mature innings for someone only 22 years old, wore their patience to the wick, and partly because sloppiness in the field contributed towards their glum demeanour. It was as though, entirely out of character, Yorkshire had begun to feel a bit sorry for themselves. Not any more.

The slow and steady strategy, which Middlesex relied upon at the beginning, was based on not losing. Their hope was that Somerset wouldn't win either, so bringing the title to Lord's. Yesterday, given the significance of the match, the two-paced pitch and the stacked cloud, their grinding out of a score was necessary for them but occasionally tedious for us.

Now tentativeness, which is entirely different from painstaking caution, has taken over. Middlesex look scared that the pitch or the ball or the bowlers possess something devilish in them. Gubbins, so sure of himself 24 hours ago, strains to get a shot away. He's pegged onto the crease, his footwork never remotely as nimble as it has been. After one inelegant push, he's rapped low on the front pad and survives an lbw appeal against Tim

Bresnan. It takes him four overs to scratch out another run. He doesn't last much longer. Bresnan gets a ball to leave him, and Gubbins – after five and a half hours of calmly determined resistance – darts after something he'd previously have left alone. The edge this time is indisputable, the catch going at stomach height to Adam Lyth at second slip. 'Tell 'em you didn't hit it, Gubbins', is the call from somewhere.

The conditions – a hot sun and a flattish surface – ought to suit Middlesex, for whom a total even of 300 would count as underperforming. So far only a laborious 36 have been added. James Franklin attempts to wrest the initiative back from Yorkshire with a couple of fours, one streaky and another briskly sublime through the covers, before becoming another Bresnan victim. The delivery he nibbles at is straighter and fuller than Gubbins', and the catch behind is regulation, swallowed by Andy Hodd's gloves. At 244 for 7 Middlesex aren't exactly in crisis, but do flounder as fortune's wheel turns towards Yorkshire. There's only some mopping-up to do.

Enter Jack Brooks, the sort of bowler you don't want to rouse to hostility. Brooks is very much in the Bresnan mould, always giving more than he has. He's intelligent, too, his wickets seldom coming through brute effort alone. The first to go is Toby Roland-Jones – another edge, another catch for Lyth. The second is Tim Murtagh, playing in the game because of the common sense and generosity of Ireland, who are allowing him to go to South Africa for a one-day series after the rest of their squad. Murtagh lasts eight balls, none of them producing so much as a single. Brooks goes around the wicket to the left-hander, spearing the ball in to cramp him. Murtagh steps towards leg, a doomed ploy, and attempts to tonk Brooks over extra cover. With an intent of menace he winds himself up in a way reminiscent of Garry Sobers during his unbeaten 150 here for the West Indies against England in 1973 (Sobers puffed out his cheeks, leant back and pyrotechnically dismissed Bob Willis from his presence). In execution Murtagh unsurprisingly lacks Sobers' polished technique. The shoulders come through the ball, but the bat turns slightly in the hand, achieving neither power nor direction. Andrew Gale takes a tumbling catch at wide mid-off.

The last Middlesex wicket arises from a combination of luck and awareness. Shortly before lunch Steven Finn, who has already swatted one four, tries to take further advantage of Brooks, who dangles a delivery outside off. The ball takes the top end of the bat and goes high to Hodd's right hand. He's like a goalkeeper, attempting to reach a free kick arrowed between the angle of post and bar. In a panicky dive he gets no more than glove-tip to it. The deflection sends the ball downwards. The next half-second seems dragged out. Lyth, alert to the second chance, leaps adroitly, his back half-turned to the wicket as Hodd's drop becomes his third catch of the innings. Middlesex are all out for 270, the collapsing rump of the innings gone in only 26 balls. With a career-best of six for 65, Brooks is given the honour of leading Yorkshire off.

There's a photograph of Lord's taken during the heyday of Edwardian England. Demure women, like figures in a Seurat painting, wear flowing white dresses to hide their ankles. Each has a dainty, veiled hat and carries an open parasol. The men accompanying them sport bird's-nest moustaches, the tips of which are waxed and twisted upward, as well as natty straw boaters and col-lared waistcoats decorated with looping, barley-twist watch-chains. Couples stroll across the outfield, posing for the purpose of social one-upmanship. It's like a fashion parade or Sunday seafront promenade. There's a bonus to being at the season's last match. We get to know how they felt. On a baking afternoon, Lord's allows us on to the outfield. The crowd can 'perambulate' – the word I once heard the velvety-voiced announcer use here – as though it's 1912 again.

Even those of us who have done this before can't resist the invitation. We step over the boundary as if reverentially entering a cathedral, and for half an hour know what it feels like to be dwarfed beside the Grandstand. I think of myself alone there beneath a catch as high as a factory chimney. I also get as close as I can to the pavilion gate, before turning and taking in the sweep of the stands. What comes to me is an image of how Lord's looks when every row is crammed, the cacophonous din of a full house in my ears. The scene is very English. The sun high and hot. The sky as blue as a child would paint it. Everyone polite. Everyone pleased to be here. *Et in Arcadia ego*.

You gain a better appreciation of the Lord's slope when you are actually walking on it. You realise as well how firm the ground is underfoot. Unlikely as this sounds, John Arlott was once pressed into emergency service as 12th man for Hampshire. He found that the outfield, which had been 'rolled and rolled and then rolled again', was harder than calcite. Next morning his feet ached, the skin sorely chafed. Your own feet, encased in new boots, would be just the same after a full shift of fielding here. Of course, photographs are taken for souvenirs. Of course, you're drawn to the square, the object of infinite fascination.

Only a month ago I'd stood next to a man behind a roped-off pitch. He'd brought his girlfriend to a game, presumably for the first time. Wanting to impress the way the love-lorn do, he'd flung himself into a monologue about footholds and block-holes, the colour and texture of disparate soils, the scuffing wear and tear a game progressively inflicts on the surface and how the outcome can pivot on it. As chat-up lines go, it was hardly Keatsian. She nodded at him, pretending to be intrigued while her eyes glazed and her thoughts drifted away.

You have to be immersed in cricket, especially in the Championship, to understand why the fanatics among us are so fascinated by the pitch and want to get as near to it as possible. It is to us what the burial mound is to the archaeologist. We are professors of cricket horticulture. We watch the scarred earth being swept, small divots replaced, sawdust sprinkled. We stare with wonder at the rake and the roller, as if such implements have never been seen before. We inspect intently spider-web cracks and shorn, pale shoots of grass, as though expecting them to grow in front us. We point and trade opinions. When we're asked to 'vacate the field' – another of the mannered phrases Lord's prefers – we do so sluggishly and only after two clangs of the pavilion bell tell us that the umpires on are on their way. A third clang obliges the stragglers to hurry up.

Yorkshire's demolition of the tail reaffirmed the difficulty of dethroning them. Middlesex can nonetheless take comfort from two things. The first is psychological. J. M. Kilburn called Scarborough 'cricket on holiday', but what Middlesex did there in the first week of July was efficiently business-like and possibly defining. At North Marine Road, one of the places of my heart, gulls wheel over a scene pleasantly unchanged since Kilburn's era. It's a shallow saucer, largely of wooden bench seating. Terraced houses sit on two sides of the ground, and in one of the backyards you're likely to see a line of washing drying in the wind. At lunch or tea I sometimes wander out of the main gate and look at the sea, following distant ships and the swells of foam as white as spring blossom. Scarborough has a magnificently ruined castle, like something from an adventure story for boys, and the grave of one of the Brontë sisters. It has candy-floss shops and trinket stores, fish and chip emporiums and neon-lit amusement arcades. It also hosts two Championship matches every summer, and Yorkshire tend to strip the opposition to the bone in front of a partisan audience, which can top 5,000.

So Middlesex's pummelling win against them there – Yorkshire lost by an innings – was foundation-shaking. On the back of it Middlesex began the surge that took them to the head of the table. Their next match, against Somerset, produced more than 1,300 runs and some barnstorming brilliance. Set 302, Middlesex teetered on 185 for 5 before flogging 96 runs off the last eight overs and squeezing home by two wickets. On his 28th birthday John Simpson blasted 79 not out from 80 balls.

We left Scarborough with the memory of Toby Roland-Jones. He struck an unbeaten 79 there, and finished with match figures of 6 for 122. In getting the ball to rear up, he demonstrated the second thing Middlesex have in their favour. If Roland-Jones or Steven Finn stood on the other's shoulders, any circus stilt-man would feel inferior. Finn is 6 foot 7 inches. Roland-Jones is 6 foot 4 inches. The extra lift and bounce their lankiness extracts is precious weaponry, particularly on a pitch such as this.

Yorkshire's top and middle order have been famished for decent scores, too. Only the openers, Alex Lees and Adam Lyth, have passed 1,000 runs. We're familiarly calm about figures flitting in and then out of the Championship again every season. Sometimes, so congested does the Test and one-day international calendar become, that plotting who is where and when requires a wall map and coloured pins.

But the door of Yorkshire's dressing room in particular this summer has been a revolving one, constantly spinning not only because of England calls but also from a shuffle of overseas batsmen. Kane Williamson was replaced by Travis Head, who was replaced by Jake Lehmann, who was replaced by no-one. Time was too tight to draft in someone new. Chop and change has worked against them. The question is whether Yorkshire can finally summon runs up front when the need is pressing. The answer comes quickly.

Everyone has had an ear cocked towards Taunton, hearing first of Somerset's fourth batting point, then their total of 365 all out and now the news that wickets have already fallen to them. Given Notts' brittleness, everyone here is braced for capitulation. What we don't expect is Yorkshire, as though coming out in sympathy, feebly folding too.

■ ■ ■

I like to watch a fast bowler side-on for a while. The way he gets to the crease can tell you a lot about him. Think of Freddie Trueman, his left shoulder dipped as though he's about to barge down a door. Think of those short, quick steps of Dennis Lillee's before he found his rhythm. Think of Brett Lee, his head poking forward so his dark, staring eyes seemed to bore clean through a batsman. At the start, Toby Roland-Jones leans into his run. He's like an old-fashioned sprinter, pushing himself out of his starting-holes. Then he snaps straight again, easing into a purposeful stride. His long legs usually cover between 16 and 18 paces, but at Old Trafford I counted one delivery at 20 and another at 21. Everything is direct, uncomplicated, un-fussy. He gets tight to the stumps, which is one of the reasons why he beats the bat often. Yorkshire can't handle him. In just 4.4 overs Roland-Jones, from the pavilion end, gets rid of three left-handers, Alex Lees, Gary Ballance and Andrew Gale, in an exemplary demonstration of the fundamentals — line, length, control — mixed in with some swing. It's as if this is a continuation of his spell at Scarborough, and that he's bowling with a mighty sea breeze at his back.

Confidence can spread fast, and then dissipate again faster still because it never takes much to bruise a man's belief in himself. This is what happens to Yorkshire. Lees spends 17 balls going nowhere before Roland-Jones dismisses him for a duck. He is partly responsible for his own downfall, sending a full ball on to the off stump after a stunted drive. Ballance has been repairing and refining his back-foot technique and also his trigger movements since an impoverished Test series against Pakistan. Seven innings brought him only 185 runs, 70 of those coming at Edgbaston. He's been batting further out of his crease and making sure his head remains stiller than before.

Roland-Jones doesn't have to do much to get his wicket, however. He simply angles the ball across him. Ballance tucks the bat almost behind his pad and, with soft hands, attempts to guide the delivery towards third man. He steers it only as far as the slips, the catch no challenge to Ollie Rayner. Yorkshire are 32 for 2. Every one of those runs belongs to Adam Lyth, who at the non-striker's end can barely look at the scene in front of him. Within another two balls, it is grislier still.

In Yorkshire's cause Gale is a pugilist, a black eye and even a sock on the jaw never enough to stop him scrapping. But no frontline batsman has had a more wretched season for them. In 26 innings he's made only 503 runs. The way he gets out now is indicative of woeful form. As Roland-Jones comes in Gale's left foot is across his stumps. His right, however, remains outside leg. The ever-so-slightly wide delivery he receives – going further down the slope – is enticing and there to attack. The Gale of 2015 would have thumped it wide of mid-off. The Gale of 2016 doesn't get to the pitch, bringing a flush of mortification to his face. The ball takes the edge. Rayner is one of those slip fielders who likes to stand with the palms of his hands resting on his knees. This time he swoops terrifically low and to his right. Roland-Jones slams his fist against the air, and Middlesex, as strangely bewildered by events as Yorkshire, whoop and holler and hug one another.

Amid the wreckage, Lyth plays as if blessed with a premonition of where every delivery is going to land. He seems to be in the right position to receive the ball a quarter-second before it is released. His cover driving is decorous, every working part of the stroke – the foot-plant, the back lift, the whip-through – superbly in sync. It's as if he's in the nets, striking balls purely for the exhilaration it brings him. Tim Murtagh gets the big stick. Lyth punishes him with three boundaries, each more accomplished than the last, the third so exquisite and venomous that Walter Hammond would applaud it. He eases himself into the shot with a liquid grace. Lyth has made 43 – nine of them in fours – off only 54 balls.

So comfortable does he look that the suddenness of his departure is startling; even he can't comprehend it. Finn, so far second fiddle to Roland-Jones, pops up something routine and just-short-of-a-length. You assume that Lyth will drive it imperiously back at him. Perhaps the height flummoxes him. Or perhaps he is late on it. Lyth plays on, hearing first the dreadful rattle of ball against bails and then Middlesex's acclaim for Finn, his arm already raised to receive it. Lyth looks back in case some awful mistake has been made, before dragging himself away with a heavy step. Yorkshire are 53 for 4.

Middlesex haven't won the title since the days of Haynes and Gatting, Ramprakash and Tuffnell and also Angus Fraser, the current managing director of cricket. That was 1993, so long ago that – unless you had access to one of the Press Association's rip-and-read machines – you had to follow the scores on Ceefax, a mode of communication so ancient to us now that it seems to belong to the age of Caxton. But in mid-afternoon, the sun blazing above the pavilion roof, Middlesex's supporters are daring to think that Championship number 13 is on the way at last. Not even Somerset's shredding of Notts – their first innings won't last beyond tea – concerns them.

On the back row of the Compton Stand, a leathery tanned and white-haired couple, dressed identically in pink Middlesex polo shirts, the sabres of the club badge stitched in darkest navy, uncork a bottle of prosecco and pour it into plastic cups. It seems premature to be celebrating; then I hear them say 'Happy Anniversary' to one another. Nearby, a group of men – mid-twenties, I suppose – raise pint pots of Marston's Pedigree and, loose-tongued from their beer, chant ''Sex – 'Sex –'Sex', a chant that in any other setting could be misconstrued.

There are two ways of tackling the position Yorkshire are in. Either go on a gung-ho fling, which could be folly, or ignore the horror of the scoreboard and start the innings again. With 50 overs to go until stumps, knuckling down is Tim Bresnan's and Andy Hodd's way of negotiating them. The partnership is like watching two craftsmen rebuild a dry stone wall. Everything is a matter of slow, circumspect placement and careful selection. Nudges. Taps. Steers. Flicks.

Never underestimate the importance of the tiny moment. The first ball Bresnan faced struck his pads, eliciting one of those brassy appeals that carries an air of entitlement, as though the umpire would be a dolt to say no to it. Bresnan was unnerved. He self-assuredly re-scratched his guard. Someone who once faced down a crowd of 90,000-plus during a Boxing Day Test at Melbourne won't be upset by the chirping of a few fielders. With such a minor gesture, he set a mood and a tone and shaped the beginning of his innings. Bresnan seems oblivious to pressure and the chasm that has opened up around him. He's disdainful of efforts to unnerve him. An out-swinger from Toby Roland-Jones arches over the shoulder of his bat. Roland-Jones throws his arms wide and then his head drops in anguished disappointment. He wants Bresnan to know how fortunate he is to still be there. Bresnan just smiles at him.

Shortly afterwards a crumpling punch of a delivery from Finn, which Bresnan seems to lose against the pavilion, belts him near the breast-bone. He briefly rubs it, but spends more time patting down the spot where the ball landed. It's a Brian Close-like act of nonchalance.

At the end of each over, the total gradually mounting, Bresnan and Hodd come together, punch gloves and chat a little. Occasionally Bresnan leans on his bat: it looks matchstick-small in his grip.

The afternoon wears on.

Hodd has three escapes. The first comes after fending away a short ball from Finn. He doesn't get completely over the delivery to stop it dead. The ball is in danger of running onto his stumps. He goes on a half-spin and manages somehow to get a toe in the way, foot out-stretched, arms flailing, like a wannabe Nureyev who can't get the hang of standing statuesquely on his points. The second, also against Finn, is a risky top-edge that drops into no man's land in front of long leg. The third is a calamity for Nick Compton.

Already, Hodd has clattered two mis-timed cuts close to the slips. Another edge, when he's on 22, travels up rather than down and goes directly to Compton. Middlesex's support is about to pop open another bottle of prosecco when Compton, as if wearing boxing gloves, puts it down. The Yorkshire fans behind him make the standard jibe about his mother catching the ball in her pinny. James Franklin, chin cupped in the palm of his hand, looks more rueful than Rodin's Thinker. Compton lies motionless on his back, staring at the sky.

What's in the air is the smell of a fresh start for Yorkshire, who have moved from clinging on to becoming combative. There are some beefy hits from

Bresnan, a handful of reverse sweeps from Hodd. The 50 partnership comes up before tea, at almost a run a ball. The 100 partnership – and avoiding the follow-on – arrives after it. Middlesex look frayed, unsure of how to break through.

Then Roland-Jones rescues them. Hodd has swayed out of the way of his short stuff, but on 64 finds himself drawn irresistibly forward. The delivery straightens, and the lbw decision is a formality. On 169 for five, Yorkshire have still to earn a batting point.

A sense of place is important in cricket. I prefer to watch the Championship at smaller grounds because when the crowd is sparse and far-flung the Test venues, except Trent Bridge, can feel soullessly empty and slightly industrial. Every minor flurry of clapping carries a cavernous echo, and apart from a high, unvariegated sweep of plastic seating there is little to attract the eye. Such surroundings are functional but seldom charming. The pastoral is always more picturesque, and consequently always more consoling: professional sport against a paint-box landscape, green fading into blue.

Scarborough isn't alone in providing this. At Worcester you have the nobility of the 172-foot cathedral tower and the sharp point of the Glover's Needle. At Cheltenham there's the neo-Gothic loveliness of the College and a pavilion that resembles a Victorian railway station. At Colwyn Bay or Basingstoke, Chesterfield or Aigburth you're tucked away among the lazy delight of steep grass banks or tents, striped deckchairs, herbaceous borders or trees. Until most grounds became tangled in the rigmarole and red tape of Health and Safety, eliminating risks more perceived than real, you'd also find the odd, half-dozing dog to pat or an ice-cream van parked on the boundary. Were it feasible, I'd make dogs welcome at cricket again; I'd even allow them to bring their owners. Were it also feasible, which I know it isn't, I'd play more, not fewer, County matches at these homely outposts, giving the Championship a renewed sense of identity.

For the last hour today, however, I decide to swap the Compton Stand for the Mound Stand, and I find Lord's transfixing me in a way it has never done before. As the sun drops, the shadows become fantastically long and lamp-black, but the pitch remains in intense sunshine, like a lit stage. It ceases to be a battleground, on which opposing forces confront one another, and instead Nature lavishes on me a painterly chiaroscuro. At Taunton Dom Bess has taken 5 for 43 and Notts, once 91 for 2, have been bowled out for a cringe-making 133. But the combination of sun and shadow, and the white-clad figures framed against the lush grass, leaves the comfortable illusion that neither here nor anywhere else do the scores matter. For a while I forget that there is a wider world beyond what I am seeing and enjoying, here, now. One moment passes into the next, peacefully seductive. Someone bowls. Someone bats. Someone fields. The component parts become a tableau.

I am revelling in the dead calm and the late sweetness of the day when David Willey's bat becomes a threshing blade. He launches Ollie Rayner towards the pavilion and then into the Grandstand for a pair of top-notch sixes. Only when Willey is out too – lbw to Tim Murtagh – do I remember that, however gorgeous the view, Yorkshire won't be relishing it. At the close, on 235 for 6, the most precarious of tightrope walks awaits tomorrow. There's only one bonus for them. Tim Bresnan is 72 not out. In every Championship game there is always a story within a story, always a duel that captivates between a batsman and a bowler. Bresnan is the lead participant in this one.

It's him versus Middlesex now.

DAY THREE

Thursday, 22 September 2016

Middlesex	15	5	0	10	48	39	217
Somerset	15	5	1	9	44	41	210
Yorkshire	15	5	2	8	46	42	208

Attendance: 4,717

S ome cricketers impress more than others, their personality endearing them to you as much as their performance. Tim Bresnan is one of them. He's only 31, so hardly the grizzled trooper, but nonetheless there's something of the old soldier about him. The way he batted for more than three and a half hours yesterday, in gutsy pursuit of what seemed – and may still be – a lost cause, said everything about his reliable talent, but also about his nature. His equanimity stood out. He accepted the position Yorkshire were in, and managed to change it.

Bresnan had never batted as high as number five before, but he buckled himself to the crease like Conrad's Captain MacWhirr tackling the typhoon by 'facing it – always facing it'. His innings was repair work on the grandest scale.

In the past few summers Bresnan has become a favourite of mine. I care if he fails or is off form. I like his big heart and his big lungs, both of which get him through a gargantuan amount of heavy lifting. I like it that there is nothing pretentious about him. His sleeves are permanently rolled up, as if work is a moral obligation, and he is never afraid to get his hands mucky. Most of all I like the respect he pays the Championship. After his 23-Test career had finished with that horrendous Ashes drubbing in 2013-14, Bresnan didn't – as others have done – act as though he was too posh for out-grounds and festivals and modest crowds. He's the archetypical pro's pro, a certain man for a certain need, and bespoke for a crisis. This is just as well, because Yorkshire are still in one.

The weather is complicated today. One minute the sun breaks through the cloud, washing everything in its brightness. The next it is gone, and Lord's is sullen. The mathematics of the day aren't so complicated. Barring catastrophic natural disaster in the West Country, Somerset will finish off Notts, pocket a further 16 points and head the table, a heartbeat or two from the club's first title. So another three batting points, which means reaching 350, are compulsory for Yorkshire. Otherwise, not even beating Middlesex will be enough to retain the

Championship; Somerset will pip them. Naysayers and doomsday pessimists will have to be confounded too. With only four wickets left, Yorkshire have to score another 115 runs in 41 overs.

Such a mountainously steep challenge is compounded by another. Toby Roland-Jones and Steven Finn are revving up to take the new ball in only 11 overs. Even among diehard Tykes, who have brought Yorkshire Tea to Lord's, the champions are being obituarised. The consensus is that, while Yorkshire can biff the odd four and irritate Middlesex, a small miracle is needed to change the narrative of the match.

If Bresnan feels this too, he doesn't show it. Again, you appreciate the depths in him, the oaken sturdiness. He seems able to push Yorkshire's plight to some far corner of his mind and forget it. There is a serene conviction about his walk from the pavilion. There is also a casual, aw' shucks grin. He places a reassuring hand on the shoulder of his partner Azeem Rafiq, who is surely pinching himself. At the start of the season he was playing for Sheffield and Phoenix CC. When injuries and the needs of England depleted Yorkshire severely, they re-signed Rafiq two summers after releasing him. He's gone from facing Doncaster at Town Fields to facing Middlesex at Lord's, swapping the Yorkshire Premier League South for the Championship's First Division.

It's predictably Rafiq, unbeaten on 20, in whom Middlesex take an excessive interest, the hostility from

Finn designed to hassle him and starve Bresnan of partners. Repeatedly the ball is thumped in short, and Rafiq has to duck and dodge. At one such delivery, he leaps — both feet off the ground — and attempts to push the ball towards leg, succeeding only in top-edging over the slips to the boundary. Finn is disgusted. What Rafiq gets for his temerity is one more bouncer. In a kerfuffle of movement, he plays a defensive stroke that goes airborne and eludes the slips for four more. Finn becomes irater still and starts talking to himself. I wonder whether he's mouthing Freddie Trueman's gruff complaint about a bat that has 'more edges to it than a broken piss pot'.

What happens in his next over, also against Rafiq, makes Finn apoplectic. In his stance Rafiq holds the bat high, as though about to replicate Victor Trumper's jump down the pitch, which George Beldam immortalised with his camera. So when Finn sends down his umpteenth short ball, just outside the line of off stump, Rafiq believes only a minimal adjustment of the wrists will slap it towards third man. It comes on faster than he anticipates, hurrying him into a dreadful mistiming. The shot takes off towards Nick Compton (the ball seems to have a certain fondness for following him). At fly slip he makes a hash of it. He's like someone trying to catch a chicken by collapsing on top of it. The drop is as bad as, if not worse than, yesterday's. Compton looks wretched. Finn looks as though he could spontaneously combust.

As though abusing Middlesex's generosity, Rafiq begins to use up his quota of lives for next season too. James Franklin, on from the Nursery End, drifts his left-arm seam across him. Another catch, easy enough, goes begging: Ollie Rayner can't hold it in outstretched hands.

After Roland-Jones is summoned to bowl at him not even the spice of the new ball prevents Rafiq from reaching his half-century with an angled dab. With the focus on him, it's as though Bresnan is allowed to move without much ado through the 70s and the 80s and now into the 90s. He's been perfectly patient in establishing himself afresh, taking whatever opportunities have been offered: a steer through the gap between second and fourth slip, a cut here, a drive there, a back-foot punch. No frills. No histrionics. No indication he is experiencing so much as a scintilla of apprehension. He placidly takes Yorkshire past 250 – another batting point garnered – and then past Middlesex's first innings total too. As always, he's proficient off his legs. One shot to the midwicket boundary is poised, everything about it immaculate: a smooth, sinuous step to get in line and a wristy lash of the bat.

Now Murtagh strays on to middle and leg, and Bresnan drives him easefully – a similar stroke – to wide mid-on. There isn't enough pace in the shot to take it to the rope, so Bresnan runs three. The last run is completed at the pavilion end, allowing him to tug off his helmet, kiss the White Rose adorning it and give a celebratory wave of his bat to the Yorkshire balcony. Coming off 222 balls, this is the sixth — and most valuable — century of his career.

In that unfathomable way memory works, one thought triggering another and occasionally exhuming the past, what comes back to me is watching Bresnan here on a freezing, rain-splattered day in 2009. The MCC faced Durham, the reigning champions, in the traditional curtain-raiser, a fixture subsequently farmed out to Abu Dhabi, where almost no one watches it. Bresnan had a fuller figure then. You could say that he was well-upholstered. He bowled from the pavilion end, his slightly rocking gait and his fleshy, heavy-set body reminiscent of the village blacksmith in the film of *The Go-Between*. Starting only his fourth Championship season, he found himself caricatured as a northern, horny-handed son of toil.

Bresnan has since educated everyone about such lazy stereotyping, proving he is much more than the trusty workhorse. Craft goes with the graft. His frame is considerably trimmer, of course, but the broadness of his back, the slightly barrelled, bull chest and the thick forearms bring a physical power. Bresnan didn't figure in a Championship game until the end of May — a calf strain was the reason — and was much missed. Yorkshire have not only become dependent on him, but the side also seems to me to be incomplete when he's absent. He's emblematic of the county.

Against all well-reasoned forecasts, Yorkshire are

coasting towards their target because of him. They're 318 – only 32 runs needed now – and the partnership is a healthy 114. Rafiq is hanging on. Despite those dropped catches. Despite his assortment of other scares. Despite a thudding blow on the helmet, which ripped off his neck guard, against Roland-Jones. Rafiq is a cricketer always capable of surprising you, and he recovers from the hazy dizziness of that blow to haul Murtagh into the front of the Warner Stand for six. It's the top note of his innings. Bresnan is so set that he could probably bat until the clocks go back at the end of next month. Franklin looks as soul-sad and puzzled as a character from Ibsen. Yorkshire are rightly chuffed; but, as P. G. Wodehouse once observed, it is when you're feeling particularly braced with things in general that Fate always sneaks up behind you with a bit of lead piping.

Before lunch Rafiq, on 65, pushes down the line against Murtagh and is comprehensively beaten by in-swing. He glances back at his knocked-down off stump as though baffled. Steve Patterson soon follows, nicking Finn to Rayner, who shows that Middlesex can still catch. After lunch no one can tell whether a prod from Jack Brooks is meant as an attacking stroke or a half-check. Whatever his intention, Brooks miscalculates. He pushes a shade too prematurely at a ball from Murtagh – his bat is well away from his body – and it loops peculiarly to Nick Gubbins at mid-on. Yorkshire are 334 for nine. What was a foregone conclusion has become a test of nerve: 16 runs required off 15.2 hold-your-breath overs.

Ryan Sidebottom, the curls of his long hair poking from beneath the rim of his helmet, joins Bresnan. Sidebottom's first class average is 13-something and he has a highest score of 61. His statistics are nonetheless less significant than his temperament. Like Bresnan, he isn't the flaky sort. Also like Bresnan, he knows perspiration is the prerequisite for inspiration. But the sky is more bruised, the light more diffused, than it has been since the opening day of the match. The wind has cracked its cheeks – the flag over the Grandstand is resplendent – and a sniff and spit of rain is in the air too. Conditions favour Roland-Jones *et al.*

As the senior partner, Bresnan has to dictate tactics: whether to have a do-or-die go, attempting to resolve the issue with a few lusty swings, or trust in Sidebottom's defence. No-one but cricket's historians can usually identify the match, but everyone knows what George Hirst is supposed to have said to number eleven Wilfred Rhodes as the pair came together at the Oval in 1902 with England needing 15 to beat Australia in the Ashes Test: 'We'll get 'em in singles'. It's one of those apocryphal yarns that repetition alone has made true. Because of our reluctance to ruin it even Hirst's categorical rebuttal to the *Leeds Mercury*, published decades later, didn't kill the quotation off.

Getting 'em in singles would be an astute plan for Yorkshire now; but they will have to be dug out. Franklin is dragging his field in, encouraging the hit over the top. Bresnan looks around him like a cartographer surveying an unfamiliar spread of land. Sidebottom assiduously practises They-Shall-Not-Pass defensive strokes. The Middlesex fielders, waved into position by Franklin, who then makes calibrated adjustments, are hunched and expectant as predators awaiting prey.

One of the definitions of 'tension' in the *Shorter Oxford English Dictionary* is: 'an immense sense of uncertainty or expectation, suppressed excitement'. This does not express by a country mile the tension that has descended on Lord's. The silence, just before every ball, is so absolute that you could hear a dropped glass break in the far distance.

In mid-August 1981, that summer of Botham and the Miracle of Headingley, Championship rivals Notts and Sussex met at Trent Bridge. The last session of the last day was played in light so murky that you almost needed a miner's lamp to see it. Notts, the leaders, were nine wickets down. In second place, Sussex knew that only a few more overs would be bowled before the umpires took the teams off, never to return.

I arrived late. The gates were open to allow anyone to come in free. I settled into a seat in the top deck of the Radcliffe Road End, staring down the line of mid-on. Possessed with a furious energy, Imran Khan tore into

Mike Bore, whose capabilities as a run-gatherer were so modest that he'd end his career with an average of 8.24. He batted more out of habit than belief. The title of John Barclay's evocative book, *The Appeal of the Championship*, is a pun on what happened that afternoon. Imran hit Bore's pad. Sussex's appeal – coming from every one of their team, irrespective of where they were fielding – was like a gas explosion. I was convinced then – and I remain so now – that Bore was out. The umpire disagreed. Notts held out for 4.4 overs before bad light gave them a draw that felt like a win, and then went on to become champions. Those of us who were there won't forget the closing stages. You had to be brave to look; some weren't and didn't.

As a veteran of that conflict, I can tell you it has nothing on this one. After each run, and after every delivery that beats the bat or hits the pad, we glance from pitch to scoreboard, as though it's about to tell us something that we don't already know. How slowly a moment can go. Overs seem elongated. Runs, picked off mostly in Rhodes-and-Hirst-like singles, come after calculation and deliberation. You want this palpitating anguish to end and you also want it to go on.

Right leg a long way forward, nose over the ball, Sidebottom is playing one watchful, model forward-defensive stroke after another. He's as orthodox as a Victorian batsman photographed in K. S. Ranjitsinhji's *Jubilee Book of Cricket*. He has cultivated the Art of the

Leave, letting the ball go with a semi-raised bat and a nod, as though wishing it well on the way past. And his husbandry of the pitch is conscientious, if only because the *tap-tap-tap* of the bat is therapeutic for the nerves.

So it's a surprise when Steven Finn bowls a short ball, and Sidebottom flounders, his air shot like watching someone flap at a wasp with a dish rag. He grins afterwards, thankful clumsiness got him nowhere near it. Finn grins back. When Sidebottom does manage to get the ball away, he completes a run like someone just pleased to get home safely. Every block is cheered, every scoring shot applauded. When Bresnan takes a swipe at a delivery from Murtagh, there is a frenzied commotion. The hit isn't out of the middle, but it clears midwicket on gusto and goes to the boundary in a succession of bouncy hops. The scoreboard ticks again when Roland-Jones only half-stops a Bresnan drive, the mis-field a gift.

The sky is pressing darkly down on Lord's now, and the prospect of rain – and perhaps a lot of it – persuades cowards such as me to abandon the top tier of the Compton Stand and head for the lower deck of the Edrich Stand. I plonk myself behind someone in a zipped fleece, the collar upturned, and straw trilby that is the colour of wheat. The neck of a wine bottle – Oyster Bay Sauvignon Blanc – is poking from his rucksack, a treat for later on. Sidebottom edges Finn. The catch hurtles towards second slip. There's a despondent moan from Yorkshire and then an agonised *arghhh* from Middlesex. The ball drops two feet short of Franklin. The man turns to me, grateful to speak to anyone within earshot, and pats his hand against his heart: 'Can't take much more of this,' he says. 'I'm a bloody wreck'.

Somehow Yorkshire have reached 349. Sidebottom has made only two in 34 deliveries when Roland-Jones gets a delivery to come back, striking him at the bottom of the pad. Like Imran and Sussex a quarter of a century ago, Middlesex think the decision isn't in dispute. The accompanying appeal is vehement and prolonged in the sure and certain belief that Sidebottom is out, the ball uprooting his middle stump. But the justice of a claim should never be assessed by the vigour with which it is expressed. What Rob Bailey hears is the whisper of an inside edge. He shakes his head and Roland-Jones rolls his eyes. The closeness of that call, and the two-second wait for confirmation of Sidebottom's reprieve, is too stressful for the man in front of me. He pulls the Sauvignon Blanc from his bag, unscrews the top and takes a swig from the bottle.

Almost immediately the light deteriorates further, making early afternoon seem like twilight. Out comes the meter. Off go the players. Yorkshire still need one run. In response to this precipice twist in the drama, the man works himself into a semi-rage. He stands up, cups his hands to his mouth in a megaphone shout: 'No ... Come back!' Ignored, he sags into his seat again exhausted. The forecast for the afternoon is 'fine and sunny'. So within five minutes something more than a heavy shower, but not quite a downpour, has swept in. It is proof England will always have too much weather, and also that no-one – least of all the Met Office – can ever predict what it will be.

The covers are on, plastic tubes gushing water into the outfield where puddles are already forming. More water is running off the top deck of the Edrich Stand. Through the hard fine rain the pavilion resembles a galleon motionless at sea, the flags limp and soggy against the jack-staff. There's nothing to do except check on the score from Taunton and sip tea so hot the cardboard cup may singe my fingers. Somerset declared their second innings on 313 for five – a second century of the match for Chris Rogers – and have already taken two Notts wickets for next to nothing. The people around me open books (though not Herodotus), unfold newspapers or tune in to the radio commentaries, swopping tit-bits of intelligence and knowing now that a draw here is useless for both teams. Somerset are sure to win today.

I don't exactly know why – is the atmosphere condu-cive to nostalgia? – but I dwell on the first, fleeting time I came to Lord's. It was 41 years ago, a hottish August, when coincidentally the match pitted Middlesex against Yorkshire. A place seldom lives up to your dreams of it. Lord's then wasn't as stately as it is now. I had expected something magically opulent. What struck me instead was its dowdiness, which the loveliness of the day seemed curiously to exacerbate: the blistered white paint and the unpointed brickwork at the back of the Grandstand, the drooping begonias in the Harris Memorial Garden, gasping for water; the accumulation of rubbish near the Tavern. I saw no more than a snatch of play late in the afternoon. Geoffrey Boycott was already on his way to making a big score, which allows me to say about him what Harold Pinter said about his hero Len Hutton:

> *I saw Boycott in his prime*
> *Another time, another time*

This wasn't the Boycott capable of grinding down bowlers the way water grinds down rock. It was a fancy innings, expressive and fluent. The imperishable image I have of him is a square drive off the back foot, the ball pinging off the sweet spot and accelerating down the slope until it cracked, like a pistol shot, against the advertising boards. Boycott tugged at the peak of his cap, a business-like gesture. Like Neville Cardus, I wasn't at ease in my surroundings that day. I felt like someone clutching a second-class ticket, afraid that he's wandered by mistake into a first class compartment. I was always expecting a tap on the shoulder, the order to move on or clear off. Lord's intimidated me as much as it did George Orwell, who watched Eton against Harrow in 1921 and later confessed to his diary: 'At that time I should have felt that to go into the pavilion, not being a member of the MCC, was on a par with pissing on the altar, and years later would have had some vague idea that it was a legal offence for which you could be prosecuted'.

My apprehension about the place has stayed with me. At the start of this season, though entitled to be at the *Wisden* dinner in the Long Room, I still expected refusal at the door when I showed my invitation, which was crowned, like the *Almanack*'s sun-bright jacket, with Eric Ravilious's engraving of those two top-hatted gentlemen. Cardus came to adore even Lord's' unswept corners, proving no one is more fervent than the convert. He became so smitten that Lord's overtook Old Trafford in his affections. He wrote valentines to the ground and announced that its name was 'graven' on his heart. I've never been completely comfortable at Lord's. Until now.

The writer J. B. Priestley reflected on those bursts of bliss – 'the moments', he called them – that are 'a prize' in life from 'God knows where'. Priestley said he suddenly knew the 'greatest happiness always when there was no apparent reason for it'. Out of nowhere it floated up to him. For Priestley, it happened once while walking through a snowstorm along Piccadilly and then across Leicester Square. He felt 'a kind of ecstasy,' he said, which he couldn't explain.

I am experiencing one of Priestley's 'moments', the 'greatest happiness' made treasurable because of the ludicrous incongruity of it. Drinking tea. Listening to the splash of lukewarm rain. Looking at swards of sopping wet turf. Waiting for the match to re-start. Maybe it's the company, this union of cricket-lovers, every one of us devoted to the Championship. Maybe it's the fond, warm memory of last evening's ravishing sunshine and shadow, the civility of a scene so quintessentially English that Housman or Edward Thomas could have written a poem about it. Maybe it's simply the thrill and intrigue of the game. Whatever the reason I am sublimely content, lost in a sense of serenity. Even if there's not a ball bowled for hours I don't want to be anywhere else but here.

The rain goes as swiftly as it came. Not so long ago, before improved drainage and the invention of machinery that simultaneously beats, sweeps and mops, there'd have been no play until after tea. But as the blue of the sky reappears, stretched like a bolt of silk, and the sun dries the field, after an interruption lasting only 68 minutes, the match re-starts. In the dressing room Tim Bresnan, apparently as laid-back as it is possible to be, has taken a nap. As he and Ryan Sidebottom return in search of that solitary run two white butterflies chase one another, as if playing a game of tag. The concrete steps of the upper tiers of the Edrich and Compton Stands glisten darkly, and you have to wipe down your plastic bucket seat before sitting on it. Yorkshire have come far, taking baby steps most of the way, but there's still the possibility that one fluky delivery – jumping up, cutting back, shooting along the floor – could undo them.

James Franklin tosses the ball to Ollie Rayner at the Nursery End. The field is a suffocating ring. Immediately Bresnan is beaten outside off stump, his attempt at a dangerous flick almost producing a thin edge. He's then beaten again playing a defensive stroke. And when Rayner, who doesn't apply much rip, twice loses his line, straying from middle and off, Bresnan sweeps without managing to score. The spinner's maiden is a battle won for Middlesex.

Responsibility passes to Sidebottom, who is facing Toby Roland-Jones. The fast bowler re-paces his run and his studs hack at the turf energetically, as though he's beginning a dig to Australia. His face is as solemn as an undertaker's. Sidebottom looks up, blinks and rams his bat into the block-hole after taking guard. He's been batting for 54 minutes. He and Bresnan have scored 15 runs off the last 75 balls. The 76th of their partnership is quickish but slips towards leg stump and cuts Sidebottom the slack he needs. He sees the chance and then seizes it. His bat is swept convincingly across his pad. As soon as the contact is made, he knows where the ball is going – and knows, too, that the wait is over.

Sidebottom is fist-pumping the air as soon as he sets off, the run unnecessary because his shot is bound for the fine-leg boundary. To judge from the shouting and the applause, which distant ships will register, you'd think the Championship itself had been won.

The shackles come off as Yorkshire's lead sails past 100. Bresnan bangs a six off Rayner. With a stroke worthy of Hutton at his regal peak, Sidebottom deliciously fires a back-foot drive through mid-off, stupefying Roland-Jones, who can't believe a tail-ender has played something so sophisticated. Only when Sidebottom becomes too adventurous, advancing down the pitch in a mini-cavalry charge and completely misses an arm ball from Rayner, does the Yorkshire innings end, on 390. Bresnan is undefeated on 142 off 293 deliveries, an extraordinarily valiant innings spanning six hours and 35 minutes. This was his moment and he came to meet it. Gloriously, in fact.

All day Jason Gillespie has been sitting in the left-hand corner of the players' balcony, wearing a T-shirt, a large-brimmed white sunhat and a pair of mirrored sunglasses. Less conspicuously, Angus Fraser is here in a suit and a Middlesex tie, the knot slightly loose around the collar. On the basis of sentiment, as well as Yorkshire's desire to turn the title into a going-away present, more attention has been paid to Gillespie, the valedictorian.

Fraser's contribution to Middlesex, if not entirely over-looked, has been partially eclipsed this week. Fraser won't entirely mind; he's never been the ostentatious or obtrusive sort, preferring to plug away, which is how he took wickets when pitches were blandly unresponsive. Naming him two decades ago as one of its five Cricketers of the Year, *Wisden* likened his 'rather inelegant and unathletic' trundle to the wicket to 'a man trampling through a nettle-bed pursued by a swarm of bees'. Aesthetic perfection, he certainly wasn't; but the qualities Fraser exhibited in his bowling for Middlesex — wholeheartedness and 'red-faced effort' — have been exhibited again ever since he gave up the Old Black Art (correspondent of *The Independent*) for this job seven years ago. Nothing excellent is wrought suddenly, and there was a forest of clearing-away and sorting-out to be accomplished before anything positive could happen.

Fraser never overcomplicated the process of doing it, changing both the mood and the culture gradually. From second to bottom of Division Two in 2009 to second from top of Division One in 2015, Middlesex have become a team splendidly like the bowler Fraser was: unshowy, difficult to get the better of, sometimes unappreciated. After the resistance Tim Bresnan put up, Middlesex are in need of some bucking-up. But this is no side of jelly-boned southern softies. Scarborough proved that. So did Taunton. So did Trent Bridge, where a few weeks ago Notts also briefly had them on the ropes. On each occasion Middlesex slugged back, counter-punching the opposition to defeat. Even with a 120-run lead, an advantage inconceivable yesterday, Yorkshire shouldn't become lax. Somerset need only three more wickets to install themselves as Championship favourites. On present form — and because of the spin of Jack Leach — it shouldn't take them much more than half an hour. The prospect that everything here could count for nothing unless one team beats the other is concentrating the mind wonderfully.

Yorkshire draw blood quickly. His batting success behind him, Ryan Sidebottom continues the impetus with his bowling. From the pavilion end, he removes Sam Robson with only his fifth ball. The delivery cuts across the opener. Robson edges it, attempting at the last moment to pull his bottom hand away. Alex Lees, the third slip, takes the catch against his stomach. You frequently see a batsman, especially after bagging a pair, hang around, as though waiting for someone to pity him. Robson goes without demur, aware this just isn't his match. He could probably come in twice more and still not score a run. Sidebottom leans back, tilts his head skywards and gives a rebel yell. Adam Lyth jumps on Lees' back and embraces him.

I think of Arthur 'Ticker' Mitchell, part of Yorkshire's inter-war successes and described as harder than the rocks on his native Baildon Moor. Anyone taking a diving catch was met with the rebuke: 'Gerr up an' stop makin' an exhibition o' thissen'. Asked what his father would have made of modern cricketers hugging one another after taking a wicket, his son once replied: 'Well, I can't remember him hugging my mother'. I imagine Mitchell, his face like a Death Mask, tut-tutting contemptuously at the sight of Yorkshire's revelry now.

He'd be abusive about the sequel too. In the next over Jack Brooks beats Nick Compton for speed, the ball thumping against the top of off stump. Brooks's follow-through takes him on an exuberant, curved run of celebration. There are high-fives, but anyone wanting to hug the bowler has to catch him first. Middlesex are 2 for 2. There's a bulletin from Taunton. Somerset have won, crushing Notts by 325 runs. Because it was expected, and so barely counts as breaking news, and also because Yorkshire are on the rampage, the response at Lord's is muted. There are murmured comments and a few so-what shrugs. Middlesex, weevilled with doubt now, still have another 30-plus overs to survive.

Yorkshire, threatening to tear the stuffing out of the top order, find Nick Gubbins in inexorable form again. There is a soothing aplomb about him. Whatever the bowling – Sidebottom or Brooks, Patterson or Bresnan – he plays it with a bat that seems broader than anyone else's. He doesn't flinch as Sidebottom smacks him on the pad. He isn't perturbed when Patterson, producing a nasty lifter, comes close to finding the edge. He appears not to care at all when, following a mistake against Bresnan, the ball he intends to work through mid-wicket squirts to third man. With Dawid Malan, Gubbins tenaciously steals singles and ignores what doesn't need to be played. He takes his time about it too, expeditiously prevaricating with finicky preparation between balls when Yorkshire attempt to rush him. He brings up the 50 partnership, uncharacteristically for this staid innings, with a pulled six off Brooks. As the ball drops into the stand Yorkshire's supporters plead aloud for anyone to 'catch t' bugger'.

The last hour is absorbing rather than exhilarating, the innings usually progressing one quarter-inch at a time. There's nothing too flash from Middlesex: that would be ornate to no purpose. Everything is secondary to staying there, which takes a real effort of endurance. Gubbins is abetted in his goal by the pitch, which is getting easier, and by the ball, which is getting softer.

Yorkshire, who had been expecting to blow Middlesex away by now, toil on as the sun drops, sending wide shadows across the field. The heat is always a physical burden. When Gubbins takes off or pulls up his helmet to get some air to his face, you also see his furrowed expression, a sign of the mental demands on him.

Only 76 runs have come from 33 overs when Lyth bowls the day's final deliveries and extracts something unexpected. He finds the edge and is aghast as the ball slides beyond second slip, allowing Gubbins to go from 36 to 39 and Middlesex to 81. The match is anybody's, and tomorrow can't come soon enough.

DAY FOUR

Friday, 23 September 2017

Somerset	16	6	1	9	44	41	226
Middlesex	15	5	0	10	48	40	218
Yorkshire	15	5	2	8	49	42	211

Attendance: 7,408

I n the Lord's Long Room, beside the door that every home batsman goes through to pass from dressing room to pavilion, hangs one of my favourite cricket paintings. It's Albert Chevallier Tayler's *Kent versus Lancashire at Canterbury in 1906*. The title is maladroit and underwhelming, perhaps deliberately so to contrast with the luxuriant splendour of his Edwardian oil. Painted to commemorate Kent's first Championship of the 'modern' era, it captures Colin Blythe bowling from the extremity of the crease to one of Neville Cardus's boyhood heroes, Johnny Tyldesley. The pair of them have counted for a long time among cricket's illustrious dead – indeed, one of them was killed in the War fought to supposedly end all others – but Chevallier Tayler does more than forever freeze Blythe (about to pivot, his left arm hidden by his body) and Tyldesley (upright, his hands high on the handle) in a duel.

The commission came from Lord Harris, whose portrait Chevallier Tayler had earlier painted. Harris wanted Blythe to be the focus of it. He also chose the match, held during the Canterbury Festival, because Blythe had appropriately claimed eight wickets. In adhering to his brief, which meant including every Kent player on the field, Chevallier Tayler's canvas became a celebration of the County Championship, and a celebration also of what cricket is, indispensably, to the summer landscape.

Everything Chevallier Tayler needed to symbolise both was available to him. He didn't have to dress the set much, but simply recreate a game he hadn't seen. There's the clock pediment, rising decoratively from the ochre-tiled pavilion roof. There's the broad, dark trees and the white tents pitched beneath them. There's a belt of blue sky and a few frothy clouds. And there's the sunlit tower of Canterbury Cathedral, dominating the middle distance as though it had been built there to complement the ground. It's the sort of ordered, placid scene even someone with no interest in the game conjures whenever cricket is mentioned. It's also redolent of England and

Empire, which is another point Chevallier Tayler tacitly makes. The touch underscoring it is barely needed, but included anyway in case the message is too oblique. Atop one of the flagpoles flutters the Union Jack.

I own a large postcard print of *Kent verses Lancashire*. It faces the desk on which I work. I particularly like to look at the painting in the dead leaflessness of winter, when the new season seems so distant that you begin to wish your life away for it. It comes to mind now because I'm asking myself which image – and there'll certainly be one – will come to define this match, this whole Championship, this last day at Lord's. It'll be a photograph rather than something painterly, but it is going to be remembered, and in the future instantly recognisable of today's events, for sure. The setting demands it. It's hot and getting hotter, one of those pellucid days that we crave but seldom get. The struggle of this game demands it too. It doesn't seem possible to me that Middlesex and Yorkshire – but especially Yorkshire – will allow Somerset to take the title when it is there for either of them to take instead.

On the 167th day of the season, we have come to the crunch, and the size of the crowd, paying only £5 admission, reflects it. These are the sort of numbers I'm used to counting only at Scarborough, where queues for the bar or the Gents usually contain more people than at whole grounds anywhere else. There are Yorkshire supporters who, cobwebbed in sleep, left the Ridings at dawn to be here. And there are faithful Middlesex followers, well past the ridge of middle age, reminiscing already about the county's banner years in the late 70s and early 80s, in anticipation that the good old days are coming back. There are also the neutrals, who have come because a flashy climax is in the offing. Lord's is alive with expectation.

Tim Bresnan takes the ball for the first over, tugs at his shirt and hitches up his flannels. He looks so relaxed that this could be a Sunday beer-match or just something casually knockabout between friends. He bowls a maiden from the pavilion end, setting a pattern. Even early on you sense you're watching preliminary sparring. It's like the start of one of those track cycle races in which the riders set off with an aching slowness, an attempt to coax a rival into sprinting for the finish before them. Once it's established that Yorkshire aren't going to grab an early wicket and that Middlesex aren't going to wantonly chuck the bat, the pleasure of the warm morning lies in the anticipation of where this jostling for position will lead by lunch or mid-afternoon.

How Time tricks us. Sometimes loitering. Sometimes galloping. It seems an age ago that I saw Nick Gubbins in the nets on the first morning. He looks more serious now than he did then, constantly re-establishing his guard and trying to look stoic, as though this day is just like any other. At his age nothing but future lies ahead and not much past is behind him. But he'll be aware that the list of players who never won the Championship, nor came close, outstrips by a dozen country miles the list of those who did. Who knows? This chance may not come again for him.

His and Dawid Malan's tactics are based essentially on occupation. The only thing that might upset them is errant bounce, which Yorkshire aren't fully exploiting. Yes, there's the occasional scare: Gubbins is beaten outside off-stump; Malan survives a scream for lbw. No, Yorkshire don't come *that* close to dismissing either of them because fortune favours Gubbins when he miscues, a toe-of-the-bat shot clearing mid-off, and Malan, who on 41 gets more edge than middle to a drive that drops safely short of cover. Even the arrival of Malan's half-century is speckled with luck. He plays defensively back at a ball from Bresnan, gets another edge and watches it bounce between and in front of Andy Hodd and first slip before scuttling off to the boundary.

But to isolate these mistakes, and overlook the substance of the stroke-making, would do a disservice to both of them. Gubbins whips Bresnan off his pads and through mid-wicket with a lovely pendulum-like swing. His fifty arrives with a punched drive through point off the same bowler, the crisply solid sound the shot makes endorsing the craftsmanship of the bat-maker. In this intensely bright light Malan is detecting anything a millimetre wide or wayward as though his retinas are radar. One drive off Ryan Sidebottom, also through point, is savagely good. Another, after taking a big, assured stride forward, is sumptuously attractive; you gasp at the glint of it.

In this way Gubbins and Malan pass seminal stages of the innings: overtaking Yorkshire's lead, reaching their hundred partnership and going on, still untroubled, to 150. Yorkshire will have seen themselves striking quickly and then sweeping through Middlesex like a scythe, leaving 200 or so as a target and enough of the day's overs left to reach it methodically, each run simply ticked off. But the best imagined plans can go awry, and the bowlers – even Bresnan, usually cheerful in the midst of battle – begin to seem a little woebegone.

If you could sneak him on to the field in disguise and under a *nom de guerre*, there is one bowler at Lord's who'd be capable of reviving Yorkshire. In a Nursery End net Shane Warne, wearing well-pressed whites, is deceiving an assortment of amateur batsmen. The run-up, the roll of the shoulder and the snap-flick of the wrist are recognisable. I still assume my eyes are lying to me, creating a mirage in the sunshine of late morning, until I get close enough to know that Warne is real and also really there.

A week ago I saw on a large screen the skeletal frame of S. F. Barnes, aged 80, during his testimonial match, a cap squeezed on to his head and a cable-knit sweater hanging off his bony body. Barnes was unable to resist bowling one over and then another, partly for the benefit

of the cameras but chiefly because, despite his rheuma-
tism, he wanted to turn his arm so much.

Warne is Barnes. He can't stop bowling either and so
probably never will. Within five minutes, there's a gaggle
of us pressed against a rail, temporarily abandoning
Gubbins and Malan and the Championship to concentrate
on Warne, fascinated even when he does nothing but
spin the ball from palm to palm. What we see is bowling
as enchantment.

Earlier in the summer I'd caught by chance his
tutorials about leg spin. Grip. Flight. Hand position. It
was as if Pythagoras had suddenly appeared to explain his
theorem and other mathematical mysteries. A few
months later on holiday, inspired by his example, I
bought a cricket ball from a traditional sports shop on the
West Sussex coast. The village in which I was staying had
a thriving cricket club. The small ground, like the village
itself, had sown islands of wild flowers, the heads of
poppies and corncockle and foxgloves colourful above
long grasses. Anyone could walk up and use the net. So I
did. I tried to follow what I remembered of Warne's
instructions, taking the ball and bowling ten overs. My
old shoulder creaked like new leather, but I was pleased
to turn a few and get the odd googly almost right. No one
laughed, which was something.

The sight of Warne at Lord's, informally chatting as
he bowls, takes me back to that village, which in turn
provides another reminder of why I love cricket so

much. Why, indeed, I'd gladly idle away entire drowsy summers at Canterbury or Hove, Worcester or Taunton. Once at Chesterfield I heard Lee Daggett, the Northamptonshire bowler, patiently answering questions about the state of the pitch from a group of spectators, each of them old enough to have voted for Clem Attlee. Daggett was fielding on the boundary and shared his intelligence with them kindly. I thought then what I am thinking now: that the sort of people who play cricket and the sort of people who watch it are as a rule very decent folk indeed. This is a companionable, salt-of-the-earth game.

The scoreboard has barely moved in the quarter of an hour I've spent watching Shane Warne, who is *still* bowling. The sun beats on, making sunscreen and sunglasses compulsory. Another pair of white butterflies – or perhaps the same pair seen yesterday – drift by, once more giving the impression that we've ripped the wrong month off the calendar. It can't possibly be September.

There's barely a spare seat in the Compton Stand now, where the weapon a Yorkshire crowd always carries – a sharp tongue – is increasingly evident. The sledging stems from agitation. Their own team's inability to make headway is one thing; Middlesex's crawl-cum plod is another. The runs come in a drip, which annoys them. 'Do yer want to win this Championship?' is one shout as Gubbins pats three consecutive deliveries back to Steve Patterson. 'Get on wi' it, Middlesex. It's not a five-day game,' is another, a joke edged with desperation.

We swap the spin of Warne for the spin of Azeem Rafiq. On the opening morning, practising on one of the old pitches, Rafiq got the ball to appreciably turn. Jason Gillespie took every delivery in a baseball mitt after a nifty side-step. But when Rafiq bowled in the first innings the surface was unresponsive, giving him no purchase. He was like an angler, optimistically casting and re-casting the same line into stagnant waters while knowing, deep down, that he'd catch nothing. With two overs to go before lunch, and Middlesex on 200 for two, Rafiq and Yorkshire are anxious for any small mercy.

Finally, it arrives. Gubbins is 93 and Dawid Malan is 99. All bets on centuries for both of them are off. Rafiq comes in and tosses the ball towards Gubbins, not expecting much as a consequence. Gubbins can glance it anywhere on the leg side. He's simply too eager, attacking so early that a leading edge gives the softest of return catches. Neither batsman nor bowler quite believes it.

It does seem that Fate, though dithering about whom to bless here, has already given Somerset the thumbs down. The last thing out of Pandora's Box was hope, which is all they have left. You can't help but muse on their players, who'll now be gathered in the 1875 Suite at Taunton to watch every ball and waiting, spectators like everyone else, for Middlesex or Yorkshire to make the decisive move. Chris Rogers, their skipper, announced his domestic retirement yesterday, aged 39. The seasons he spent at Lord's, the last of them as captain, are a piquant sub-plot to today's outcome.

Most of us, however, talk about Marcus Trescothick. He'll be 41 on Christmas Day, began his career at Somerset as far back as 1993 and has been a Championship runner-up three times. Earlier in the summer I saw him score a double hundred against Notts at Trent Bridge. The pitch was cut towards the side of the ground where George Parr's tree stood before a storm blew it down almost four decades ago (Notts made miniature bats from the splintered wood). As a boy I sat in front of that tree beside the Windrush generation: West Indian men in smart slim suits, narrow ties and pork-pie hats who, like me, were there to worship Garry Sobers.

I got as close as I could to my old spot, admiringly following Trescothick, who bats in spectacles these days. His driving was fierce; majestic shots from such a powerfully majestic batsman. The ball went from bat to boundary straighter than a Roman road. Early on Luke Fletcher, the Notts bowler, thought Trescothick had edged a ball. When the appeal was rejected, he stomped up to him in the crease and for a minute or so the two them – Fletcher 6 foot 6 inches tall, Trescothick 6 foot 3 – were face-to-face, exchanging pleasantries about the nice weather, no doubt. Afterwards Trescothick went hotly on. Many of his princely strokes obliged Fletcher to pursue them like a punishment.

It's been ten years since Trescothick's last Test appearance. It's been eight since the publication of his autobiography *Coming Back to Me*. The importance of that searing book, essential in any cricket library, can't be over-stated because it inspired – and still does – discussions about mental illness, thus de-stigmatising it. In the improbable event that Middlesex and Yorkshire don't come to some arrangement this afternoon, or if one fails to knock the other out after that arrangement is struck, no one will begrudge him his Championship medal. For Trescothick not to own one seems unjust; you want to protest about it or raise a petition.

The first completed business of the afternoon is Dawid Malan's century. Azeem Rafiq's third ball – a delivery not dissimilar to the one that got Nick Gubbins into such a shemozzle – is clipped to mid-on, and Malan covers the ground at quicksilver speed. After the applause dies away, and Malan deservedly milks it, there's the expectation that Middlesex will give Yorkshire a severe dressing-down, setting them a total to chase at last. Instead, Steve Eskinazi, Malan's new partner, takes 27 deliveries to get off the mark. It's as though something he ate at lunch is lying heavily on his stomach. One corpulent chap in a flame-red baseball cap, his grey sideburns and eyebrows as stiff and protruding as the bristles of a scrubbing brush, starts to complain about 'giving this game up as a bad job' and heading to a pub. Another, sitting almost directly behind me, gripes incessantly about everything.

Cricket fans can be an odd bunch; idiosyncratic on occasions and sometimes downright eccentric. I remember a woman knitting a crimson scarf longer than Jimmy Anderson's run. I remember a man, his face as veined as a leaf, who'd written out the tables and the first-class averages on to scraps of paper and cardboard. He produced them on request, answering queries about this batsman or that bowler with a Frindall-like authority and intonation. I remember someone in half-moon spectacles at Worcester, observing each delivery in between reading e e cummings' *Complete Poems*, the hardback breeze-block thick.

I remember another man, aged 70-something, laying a scorebook across his knees at Cheltenham, where every ball was recorded in coloured pencils with the meticulousness of a copper-plate engraver. Most of all, I remember this season a curmudgeon who, during the morning of the Roses match at Old Trafford, damned every aspect of Yorkshire cricket and Yorkshire life as though holding a grudge that dated back to the Act of Accord. I didn't think I'd ever again be in the presence of such a malcontent.

I was wrong. My neighbour today could be his cantankerous cousin. 'Match is rubbish ... Middlesex don't deserve 'owt anyways . . . bloody Yorksheer can't bowl . . . don't know why I came 'cos it only means going home again'. These are idiot snarls. He doesn't appreciate that Middlesex are waiting to be wooed; waiting, in fact, for Yorkshire to ask them to dance.

At five to two drinks arrive, the camouflage of tray and glasses fooling no one. Messages are being passed and Yorkshire huddle together, a conclave of talking heads. Even with binoculars I can't lip-read everything being said, but I can guess most of it. Calculations are being made. There are 52 overs remaining; Middlesex's lead is 104. Ten minutes later, after Malan and Eskinazi have added another 15 runs, Andrew Gale slips off the field, trying not to be conspicuous about it. This is difficult when everyone is looking; he must feel our gaze upon him like a hand. His stride lengthens as he nears the pavilion gate, anxious to complete the off-stage bartering with James Franklin. There's a hum throughout the crowd. I think again of Somerset and Marcus Trescothick, helpless but trying to be philosophical at the same time.

Gale returns and another, much briefer conflab takes place before Adam Lyth starts to sacrifice his bowling figures for the greater good. The game is on, but the free runs Lyth gives away are as easy to collect as windfall apples and ought to have asterisks alongside them in the averages. What leaves his hand is long hops, donkey drops and half-volleys. All sorts of dross is offered and gratefully accepted, making scoring easy and quick. Eskinazi helps himself with lavish drives and hard pulls. Five fours and a two come off Lyth's first over.

Yorkshire's main bowlers spread themselves in likely places around the outfield. Alex Lees comes on instead of them. He's bowled only six first class overs before. He's never taken a wicket. He knows what to do, but isn't entirely sure how to make it interesting.

J. M. Barrie, preserving the Peter Pan streak within him, liked to bowl for the team he formed, a celebrity XI called the Allahakbarries. At 5 foot 3 inches, and built as though his entire frame was made from chicken wire, he was no great shakes as a cricketer. He once told Neville Cardus that his deliveries were 'so slow' that 'if I don't like a ball I can run after it and bring it back'.

Lyth bowls slower than Barrie ever did; and Lees bowls slower than Lyth, which must possibly make him the slowest bowler even seen at Lord's. One delivery in particular to Malan is so dreadful that you could enjoy a two-course lunch with wine in the time it takes to float from crease to crease.

A thousand and one thoughts must be rioting in Malan's mind as the ball dollies towards his leg stump. Not only is Lees asking to be hit clean over the Grandstand, he is also giving Malan the chance to smash the ball further than the last of Sobers' six sixes at Swansea, which disappeared out of the ground and down the High Street. Malan, on 116, can't resist trying. Like someone swinging a hammer at a fairground test-your-strength machine, he gives the shot all he's got. *Bang*.

It zooms off the bat – and straight to square leg. Jack Brooks takes it in his right hand without moving from the spot. In the whole history of first-class cricket someone, somewhere must have bowled a ball even worse than this one and taken a wicket, but you're still tempted to ask for nominations to confirm it. The crowd dissolves into derisive laughter. Considering what we've already seen, Lees to Malan to Brooks is no more than a scratch on the surface of the match. We aren't, however, ever likely to forget something so comically slapstick, a gracious innings ending with the batsman slipping on one of the game's banana skins.

So it goes on. The bowling gets worse and is thumped to all parts. The only longueur, amid the tumultuous motion of everything, is the fetching back of each delivery. John Simpson makes 31 off ten balls – six fours, one six – before Lees takes his second wicket, clean bowling him. Franklin arrives and claims six fours of his own. Eskinazi, as if an alarm clock has gone off next to his ear, sweeps past 50 and into the 70s. In nine overs Middlesex make 119. Amid this bang and clatter you're left asking yourself, like the impatient child on the back seat of the car, whether we are 'there yet'. Lyth has conceded 77 runs in 7.5 overs; Lees 51 from four.

Eventually, on 359 for six, Franklin declares with good manners. Rather than slashing another tame ball from Lyth for four, he clips it up in the air for him. It's like a soft lob in tennis. Lyth has only to take a few shuffling paces to his right, the catch plopping into his hands. Franklin is walking off even before Lyth completes it, waving Eskinazi in with him.

Yorkshire need 240 to win in 40 overs.

The cricket aficionado and Booker-shortlisted author J. L. Carr was at Headingley in 1932 when Yorkshire faced Notts. His brother-in-law 'prophesied rain,' he said. The two of them caught the train home to Sherburn-in-Elmet and so missed Hedley Verity take 10 for 10, figures of symmetrical perfection unmatched before or since. 'This blighted my youth,' said Carr. I glance around Lord's, during an early tea that means Yorkshire's innings will be uninterrupted, but can't see the man in the flame-red baseball cap. Perhaps he did leave early and is in a pub now. Perhaps, like Carr, he will forever regret it.

There have been a few epic final-day finishes to the Championship in the last few decades. In 1977 Gloucestershire were comfortable favourites until Hampshire, near the bottom of the table, astonishingly beat them, a result allowing Middlesex and Kent to share the title. In 1984 Notts, with one wicket left, needed 14 off the last over against Somerset. From the first three balls Mike Bore (yes, him again) hit four, four and two. The fourth was blocked. The fifth, swung high towards the boundary, was caught two feet from the rope. The beneficiaries were Essex, who became champions by 24 inches.

And in 2010 Notts – again – needed six bonus points at a damp Old Trafford and got them, forcing a draw to edge out Somerset – who else? – on the basis of winning one more game than them. None of those matches possessed the sustained, see-saw melodrama of this one. It's the best possible publicity for the beleaguered institution that, for want of tender loving care, the Championship has become.

The competition has periodically undergone convulsive change. In format and size. In rules and regulations. In upswings and downswings of fortune. It's only to be expected in something created when Queen Victoria was still mourning Albert. Most of this change was well-meaning restoration, meant to maintain the essential fabric. In this way, even after its split into two divisions, the Championship has somehow always moved on and always survived. Whether it can again is doubtful now; for a parlous state is becoming a perilous one. Next summer the Championship will get another hard shake, shrinking from 16 to 14 matches per county. This doesn't sound much until you do the maths. Division Two becomes lopsided, too, a cockamamie Heath Robinson-like contraption in which not all the teams will play one another home and away. There will, at least, be the restoration of Saturday Championship cricket, reminding us how plainly stupid scrapping it was in the first place. We are grateful but not completely reassured. For in a season soon to come, more Twenty20 will be wedged into the over-crowded summer, the long-term repercussions so obvious as to require no elaboration.

What's presently going on is the incremental disman-tling of the County Championship, until the opposition (i.e. people such as me) are resigned to the inevitability of the outcome, thus chucking in the towel. The ECB has a parental duty of care, but the message that comes across to me subliminally in all that's done and said under-mines the competition as an anachronistic nuisance, filling up umpteen weeks that Twenty20 can use more profitably. Talk about friendly fire. Imagine if English Heritage began bulldozing stately homes, arguing that their upkeep was too bothersome and not nearly lucra-tive enough. No doubt, far into the future, someone will say sorry for all this.

When Twenty20 began, I loathed it. I loathed the slogging, the repetitive thud of the music after the fall of a wicket, the way everything seemed so gauche and forced, like someone constantly blowing a party horn in your face. I particularly loathed the commentators who, hyping everything up to showbiz hoopla, gave a banshee wail after even the banality of a leg-bye. It left them nowhere to go on the vocal register when a wicket fell or a shot went out of the ground.

But the liberty we all have is to change our minds;

aren't our heads round so our thoughts can change direction? I changed my mind on the basis of emotions, not facts. It happened as Twenty20 became less crude and more sophisticated. There were new shots, new deliveries and new tactics, and I began admiring in isolation the skills needed to master them. But I still prefer a day at the Championship to a floodlit night of Twenty20.

Neville Cardus never saw a lot of merit in the Gillette Cup, and even less in the John Player League. So, as a connoisseur of classical music as well as cricket, he'd regard Twenty20 as the equivalent of someone attempting to play Elgar on a dustbin lid. Cardus, however, never opposed the one-day game purely on personal taste. He was more practical than that. He believed that you had to maintain a robust Championship to maintain a robust Test team. Think of it as like a penny farthing bicycle, the small wheel stabilising the big one.

The debate about that will go on, but here and now – as Middlesex are about to bowl to Yorkshire's openers – it matters only that the Championship is a subject of interest again, holding the attention on its own merits. Newspapers, consumed by football's latest groin strain or a manager's attempt to make a platitude sound like an epigram, normally push it to the periphery of the back pages. It's been different this week. The controversy over the ECB's reforms has touched a nerve. The Championship is a news story again.

■ ■ ■

It's a match within a match now. The four-day title will be determined by a one-day contest. Fiction has to avoid endings like this to swerve around the charge of implausibility. Real life thankfully does not. There's cheering, as if this is an old-fashioned cup final Saturday at Lord's and everyone is here to have a good time whatever the result. It's the sort of atmosphere that prickles the skin. This last session of the last day of the last game will come and go in a blur, I know, and be remembered kaleidoscopically, a bright frieze of fragmentary images, each dependent on the perspective from which it is viewed. I look down and across the packed rows. All of us are hunched forward a little in our seats, pressing ourselves closer to the field.

The early exchanges are played in near silence, as if few dare exhale. Only when the bat is beaten or a stroke is made does the bellowing begin. Alex Lees doesn't score as many runs off the first over, from Tim Murtagh, as he conceded in any one of his own, but uses his height to angle the bat artfully and place, rather than power, a shot to third man. When Toby Roland-Jones comes on – from the pavilion end – Adam Lyth takes advantage of the same gap, which is as conspicuous as a missing front tooth. Yorkshire mustn't be daft about this chase, but can't afford to slouch either.

If a quick advantage is established, it belongs to them marginally. Lees locks on to a wide Murtagh half-volley, his arms swinging beautifully into and through the shot without hesitation. After five overs, the balance of attack and caution just about right, Yorkshire are whittling the target down instead of attempting to demolish it. Then Roland-Jones strikes. With the last ball of his third over, he gets one to go across Lyth, who dabbles at it irresistibly. The edge goes comfortably to Sam Robson at first slip. Yorkshire are 27 for 1.

Earlier in the season David Willey, facing Glamorgan at Cardiff, hit a whizz-bang 79 off 38 balls to take Yorkshire to Twenty20 Finals Day. It was an uninhibited exhibition of stellar hitting – most of it off a decent length. In the first innings Willey came in at number seven. Now he appears at number three. No statement of intent could be clearer. It's like wheeling out the big cannon before letting the infantry loose.

Opinion is divided. Some think Middlesex's declaration is preposterously generous, setting Yorkshire a pipsqueak score that a few lusty blows from Willey – and later on from Tim Bresnan – will overtake long before 40 overs are up. That explosive scoring against Hampshire last April is cited as clinching evidence of how easily achievable the target is. To me that is nonsense on stilts. The two batsmen who instigated it, Jonny Bairstow and Liam Plunkett, aren't playing, and Hampshire's attack was also rag-tag and weak, whereas Middlesex formidably have Roland-Jones and Steven Finn. Six runs an over on a worn, slow pitch, with the field out and the boundaries long, means Yorkshire will have to bat almost faultlessly, and do so under extreme pressure. This can't be a thrash, like an old-fashioned 40-over Sunday game, and nurdling the ball around and then running like stink won't be enough either.

Willey, proving all this, strains to make inroads. He pinches a single in one over. Murtagh ties him up in a wily maiden in the next. Since the tonic of claiming a wicket, Roland-Jones's run-up looks at least three strides longer than before. He seems quicker, too. You realise how awkward it must be to face him, the ball coming at you like something falling off a church steeple. One delivery, which could conceivably have made Bradman look a chump, whistles past Willey, who is still playing his shot when the ball is past him.

After 10 overs the required rate has inched upwards to 6.5. With no other option but to have a go, Lees tries to hoik Murtagh towards cow corner. On an out-ground, you'd find the ball in someone's front garden. On Lord's' manicured acres, it only reaches Nick Gubbins, who takes the catch just above the knee. In Yorkshire there's nowt so glum as folk.

This isn't the sort of situation in which someone scratching for form, such as Gary Ballance, wants to find himself. He barely survives against Roland-Jones, who twice strikes the pad to the accompaniment of throaty appeals. On occasions Ballance takes the odd, agitated air-swipe. If he'd connected with any of these attempts, two things would have happened. Albert Trott's six over the pavilion in 1899 would have become the second most legendary shot at Lord's; and someone in a flat on the Grove End Road would now be telephoning for a glazier. As it is, Ballance merely brings up huge puffs of dust, the toe of his bat scuffing the deteriorating surface. The harder he tries to hit the ball, the less successful he becomes. There are more swings than hits, too, from the restless Willey, unable to get into a groove. He does find the boundary with a crack – a fiery cover drive – after taking a pace and a half down the pitch to Murtagh.

It's a pyrrhic victory. Willey has made 11 off 21 deliveries when Murtagh induces him into something wilder. He plays one of those shots that seems a good idea at the time, but is actually egregious, a memory for the scrapheap rather than the scrapbook. The ball spirals towards long-on. Steve Eskinazi watches and waits and back-pedals, clutching the chance against his chest and giving a yelp of gratified thanks. On 48 for 3 in the 13th over, Yorkshire's star is glimmering out.

Bresnan is wearing his best gladiatorial expression. The eyes blink a little, but that's only to adjust to the harshness of the light. There's certainly no aw' shucks grin from him today. He begins patting down the pitch at the non-striker's end, the face of his bat still bearing some of the marks of his earlier century. For anyone else, Yorkshire's dire straits would be intimidating. For him it is merely an awkward problem to be solved.

Bresnan begins confidently, as if there's been no

hiatus between this solo performance and the previous one. You'd have thought Murtagh would know not to bowl on his legs after getting whacked over or through midwicket and mid-on regularly enough for the best part of a day. When he slides a dog-tired ball towards the pads, Bresnan takes a half-step inside the line and sends it in a predictable direction. Away the shot sails. Bresnan, the resilient core of the side, is in business again.

The rate is still on an upward curve. It's 7.8, a chokehold for Middlesex, until Bresnan slowly takes command, impressive in everything he does. Roland-Jones's strength is the precision of his deliveries, the ball always on a length and always on or near off stump. In a great burst of work, which leaves fine drops of sweat glistening on his forehead, he manages to make scoring difficult even for Bresnan. Finn, too, starts in that mean manner. One shot against him – the timing remarkable, the blow quite beautiful – nevertheless announces a marked shift of momentum. Finn drops a delivery short and Bresnan does no more than flick it off his hips. It's a forearm jab, but minimum effort brings maximum distance. The ball disappears over deep square leg for six. He, rather than Willey, ought to have come in higher up.

Even Ballance, as though something of his colleague's sang-froid is rubbing off him, begins to look surer in his own skin. He also belts a prodigious six, getting down on one knee and sweeping a ball from Ollie Rayner into the Grandstand. Bresnan barely bothered to look where his six had gone. Ballance follows the trail of his own like a golfer watching a drive off the tee. The match, which belonged to Middlesex only half an hour ago, is swaying Yorkshire's way. With 20 overs left, they need 153.

As the contest begins to spin faster, you are conscious of nothing but the next ball. You're held in the moment. No-one moves. You don't look at the clock – for time really is away and somewhere else – but only at the scoreboard, calculating and recalculating the run rate and who has bowled what. Middlesex have gone from elation to frustration and are now troubled. James Franklin appears unsure of what – or who – can rid them of Tim Bresnan and put them in charge again. If only Toby Roland-Jones could bowl inexhaustibly and at both ends at once for him.

Yorkshire are only two short of 100 when Franklin gets his break. Gary Ballance, emboldened by his earlier shot, takes an agricultural mow at a delivery from Steven Finn. Up it goes, the shine on the ball catching the sun. It seems to hang in the sky, a hard dark dot on a cobalt background, before falling. Like David Willey before him, Ballance is mortified. Also like Willey, he goes through the routine of taking a run while looking at the catch, which is heading for mid-on, where Sam Robson steadies himself under the ball and is euphoric after claiming it. Ballance is out for 30, another concussive blow.

As Andrew Gale arrives to partner Bresnan, some of

Yorkshire's supporters stand on their seats, somewhat shakily, to applaud him, making the atmosphere more passionately febrile than ever. A leader, such as Gale, is supposed to demonstrate what is still possible. At this juncture, however, he has only to pick off runs where and however he can and feed much of the strike to Bresnan, who is moving towards his half century.

The overs tick by. Some are small triumphs for Yorkshire – a cut from Gale for four, a pull from Bresnan to the boundary. Some are small successes for Middlesex – a jaffer from Finn that Gale touches and is relieved to see bisect John Simpson and first slip, an in-swinger from the recalled Roland-Jones that Bresnan nibbles on to his pad. With the prize anyone's, Middlesex pass up one opportunity that would surely make it theirs. Bresnan top-edges after audaciously reverse sweeping Ollie Rayner. Dawid Malan can't get low enough to take it, the ball grounded. Punishment for that miss is instantaneous. Bresnan spanks Rayner for a six and a four, pulling off his helmet at the end of the over and shaking the sweat from his brow. When he pushes a safe single, bringing up his fifty in 44 balls, Yorkshire need 93 off 11 overs.

We presume Bresnan will steer them home from here, the unrivalled Man of the Match. We presume someone in Yorkshire is right now prising the lid off a tin of gold paint and preparing to put Championship number 34 on the honours' board at Headingley. And we presume that afterwards Middlesex will ponder, with the advantages of hindsight, every tantalising what if and what-might-have-been. But then the game astonishes us again.

Bresnan's preference for peppering the on side takes him across his crease. A ball from Roland-Jones, which he believes is heading beyond leg, holds its line. The appeal on the field is drowned out by the appeal off it, as loud as a hallelujah. The ball would have clipped the top of middle stump. Bresnan, his shoulders hunched, goes in speechless desolation, taking with him any hope of the Championship. On 154 for 5, Yorkshire need 87 off 10 overs, the damage irreparable.

There's no attempt to block or shore up the tail to get a draw and deny Middlesex the title. Yorkshire go on blazing away, the obligation to do so surely in the fine print of the deal Gale made with Franklin before the declaration bowling began. Somerset may as well switch off the television in Taunton, where a sea of cider won't numb the sadness of being runners-up again.

Yorkshire start to sink, albeit proudly. Gale, a man whose heart always hurts in defeat, comes down the pitch to Roland-Jones and carves at a ball that dislodges his leg bail. With eight overs left – Azeem Rafiq and Andy Hodd are together – Yorkshire still need 66.

After this finishes, someone ought to put together a highlights package to be shown whenever the Championship's capacity to captivate us is doubted. For a match that has already given so much gives even more in its dying fall, a last act of derring-do no one foresees.

Anyone sceptical about the sporting term 'in the zone' has only to look at Roland-Jones to realise it isn't a myth. He is bowling with a concentrated focus that is absolute, every stride and every wrenching whirl of muscle and bone achieved apparently without conscious effort. He's supercharged, and his run-up seems to have got flamboyantly longer still. You wouldn't be surprised to see him start it from the Pavilion gate. Roland-Jones is pandemonium let loose. With the last ball of his twelfth over, Rafiq perishes in much the same fashion as Willey and Ballance. He attempts a quiver of aggression against a delivery on off stump. It kicks up, flying high off the bat. Simpson runs to the spot fifth slip would occupy, taking the simplest catch of the season.

In the next over Steve Patterson makes an enormous amount of room for himself against Finn. A full, fast delivery dynamites his off-stump. Middlesex have 30 balls to take two wickets. Yorkshire need 61 runs. Nothing remains for them except the small task of achieving the impossible.

What Roland-Jones does next leaves behind a trail of exclamation marks. With the first ball of his thirteenth over, he bowls Hodd, a cross-bat contributing to the batsman's downfall. With the next Ryan Sidebottom, his body-language implying dejection, moves inside the line and attempts to play the finest of fine glances. He loses his leg stump.

Roland-Jones has a hat-trick. Middlesex have the title. Lord's has its stupendous grand finale.

Woozy with his achievement, Roland-Jones hares off, arms out-stretched, until his team mates pile on top of him in celebration, overwhelming him with praise. The wicket he's just taken could conceivably define his cricketing life. It's a moment of complete fulfilment; and he'll be asked about it till his last breath. The air seems to shudder, and the ground becomes a bowl of noise, brimming with cheering and hollering and applause. We allow it to soak into us, and look at one another incredulously, as though waiting to be gently shaken awake and told that none of this has actually happened. Say what you like about the gerrymandering that forced it; I don't care. Out of good intentions came a thriller. There are over 7,000 people here, but I'm certain three times as many will subsequently claim attendance and convince themselves of the truth of their white lie.

'It's one of the misfortunes of cricket that the history of it has to be written largely in statistics,' wrote Neville Cardus, cursing the cold print of numerals and damned dots of the scorebook, when what memory lingers over and cherishes is colour, atmosphere, the act of fancy. That's what we'll remember from these four days. Gubbins grafting for his runs ... Bresnan's bellicose refusal to give in ... Lees getting rid of Malan so farcically ... Roland-Jones ripping in to have that final word ...

It is difficult to judge something when it is actually happening. We wait for Time and history to bring proportion and order and rank to events. But I'm certain this match will live beyond its period, the totality of the experience too durable ever to fade.

And if someone is prepared to paint it, becoming a modern-day Albert Chevalier Tayler, there's an image awaiting an immense canvas; something to preserve what's just slid before our eyes and to hang in the Lord's Long Room. It ought to be painted from the Nursery End, so the pavilion's terracotta stone is the backdrop, the cantilevered balconies full and the white flag poles almost as tall as a ship's mast. Call it *The Last Ball of the Season*, and paint it like this. A low sun flooding the field in a relucent light. Every shadow elongated, as though distorted like the reflection in a fairground mirror. Sidebottom's head down and turned slightly, his bat held limply across his torso and his leg stump flat on the ground. Roland-Jones, face phosphorescent with joy, eying the sky, his arms wide and his mouth agape half in disbelief and half in exultation. Here Kipling's twin imposters co-exist. In them you see what it means to win a Championship – and also what it means to lose one.

The presentation ceremony takes place in front of the pavilion – for the benefit of television and the MCC's membership, of course – even though the crowd are gathered at the Nursery End. It's like watching a neighbour's party from across the road. In gleaming sunshine the new Kings of Summer then go on a slow lap of honour, savouring every step and also their standing ovation. The trophy is passed from hand to hand. James Franklin kisses it. Nick Gubbins looks dreamily at the filigree inscription on it. Toby Roland-Jones raises it high. Yorkshire trail respectfully behind Middlesex, applauding those who are applauding them, trying not to look too crestfallen and proving there's dignity in honourable defeat. Only the most arid heart would feel nothing for them.

I slip away to the Print Shop and shuffle along in the queue for a completed scorecard, a little piece of souvenir ephemera hot off the press. A dozen places further on in the ever-expanding line I spot a flame-red baseball cap; so he didn't leave after all. He looks around him and I realise there really is no more fascinating surface on the earth than the human face. A Middlesex member comes past, waving the scorecard he's bought. He and a friend embrace. 'Told you we'd bloody well do it,' he tells him. We gabble amongst ourselves, reliving the implausibility of the day.

'I thought I was going to faint,' says one man.

'I don't think', rhapsodises another, 'that I've been to a match like that for . . . oh, forty years'. (Later I wish I'd asked him which match he meant).

'Poor Bresnan,' says a Yorkshireman, his voice as sad as a cello: 'The lad must be crushed'.

It's easy to come by sentimentality, but there's a twinge of wistfulness in every conversation. For we can't do this again for another six months. It'll be November before the fixtures are published. It will be late March, or perhaps the first week of April, before we'll watch cricket anywhere but on television. So we'll wait. For flowers to sprout on the roadsides. For the fields and the hedgerows to thicken. For the first sight of the swallow and the swift. And then one fine morning...

But all that seems a long way off as I go back to the top tier of the Compton Stand and take a last look over the ground, almost deserted now and swaddled thickly in shadow, the odd bird pecking at the grass.

Neville Cardus always remembered a game at Dover. Afterwards he 'stayed for a while in failing light', standing alone to mourn the passing of a season 'all over and gone'. From the well of what he felt there came one of his most quoted lines: 'There can be no summer in this land without cricket'. I think of that line and also of him, my good companion, and know I'm only delaying the inevitable. So at last, and reluctantly, I stop loitering and turn towards the Grace Gates, which is the only way to leave Lord's.

As a comfort I tell myself that I'm not walking away from this summer, but instead heading towards the next...

Middlesex	16	6	0	10	48	40	230
Somerset	16	6	1	9	44	41	226
Yorkshire	16	5	3	8	49	42	211

Scorecard

Middlesex v Yorkshire, Lord's, 21–24 September 2016

Toss: Uncontested

Umpires: R. J. Bailey, R. T. Robinson

Middlesex first innings		Runs	Balls	Mins	4s	6s
S. D. Robson	lbw b Brooks	0	15	14	-	-
N. R. T. Gubbins	c Lyth b Bresnan	125	274	370	16	1
N. R. D. Compton	lbw b Brooks	8	24	35	1	-
D. J. Malan	b Willey	22	24	26	4	-
S. S. Eskinazi	b Brooks	12	45	66	2	-
+J. A. Simpson	lbw b Bresnan	15	76	94	3	-
*J. E. C. Franklin	c Hodd b Bresnan	48	106	152	8	-
O. P. Rayner	not out	15	54	76	1	-
T. S. Roland-Jones	c Lyth b Brooks	7	19	33	1	-
T. J. Murtagh	c Gale b Brooks	0	8	15	-	-
S. T. Finn	c Lyth b Brooks	6	7	10	1	-
Extras	(4 b, 6 lb, 2 nb)	12				
Total	(all out, 108.3 overs)	**270**				

Fall of wickets:
1-11 (Robson, 3.4 ov), 2-33 (Compton, 11.4 ov), 3-57 (Malan, 17.2 ov), 4-97
(Eskinazi, 33.4 ov), 5-154 (Simpson, 56.6 ov), 6-229 (Gubbins, 92.2 ov), 7-244
(Franklin, 96.3 ov), 8-254 (Roland-Jones, 104.1 ov), 9-258 (Murtagh, 106.5 ov),
10-270 (Finn, 108.3 ov)

Yorkshire bowling	Overs	Mdns	Runs	Wkts	Wides	No-Balls	Dots	4s	6s
Sidebottom	22	12	29	0	-	-	116		
Brooks	23.3	2	65	6	-	-	111		
Willey	16	1	71	1	-	-	68		
Patterson	17	9	32	0	-	1	89		
Bresnan	23	7	48	3	-	-	117		
Azeem Rafiq	7	1	15	0	-	-	36		

Yorkshire first innings		Runs	Balls	Mins	4s	6s
A. Lyth	b Finn	43	54	74	9	-
A. Z.. Lees	b Roland-Jones	0	17	24	-	-
G. S. Ballance	c Rayner b Roland-Jones	0	4	18	-	-
*A. W. Gale	c Rayner b Roland-Jones	0	2	4	-	-
T. T. Bresnan	not out	142	293	455	12	1
+A. J. Hodd	lbw b Roland-Jones	64	104	143	7	-
D. J. Willey	lbw b Murtagh	22	27	40	2	2
Azeem Rafiq	b Murtagh	65	97	126	10	1
S. A. Patterson	c Rayner b Finn	11	20	24	1	-
J. A. Brooks	c Gubbins b Murtagh	0	4	5	-	-
R. J. Sidebottom	b Rayner	23	80	88	4	-
Extras	(14 lb, 6 nb)	20				
Total	(all out, 116.3 overs)	**390**				

Fall of wickets:
1-14 (Lees, 5.4 ov), 2-32 (Ballance, 9.2 ov), 3-32 (Gale, 9.4 ov), 4-53 (Lyth, 15.6 ov),
5-169 (Hodd, 51.3 ov), 6-204 (Willey, 60.6 ov), 7-318 (Azeem Rafiq, 88.3 ov), 8-333
(Patterson, 93.5 ov), 9-334 (Brooks, 94.4 ov), 10-390 (Sidebottom, 116.3 ov)

Middlesex bowling	Overs	Mdns	Runs	Wkts	Wides	No-Balls	Dots	4s	6s
Murtagh	32	4	96	3	-	-	149		
Roland-Jones	29	5	73	4	-	-	132		
Franklin	9	1	32	0	-	1	39		
Finn	30	4	105	2	-	2	124		
Rayner	16.3	1	70	1	-	-	65		

Middlesex second innings		Runs	Balls	Mins	4s	6s
N. R. T. Gubbins	c and b Azeem Rafiq	93	200	260	9	1
S. D. Robson	c Lees b Sidebottom	0	3	7	-	-
N. R. D. Compton	b Brooks	1	8	13	-	-
D. J. Malan	c Brooks b Lees	116	246	319	14	-
S. S. Eskinazi	not out	78	83	98	10	4
+J. A. Simpson	b Lees	31	10	6	6	1
*J. E. C. Franklin	c and b Lyth	30	14	17	6	1
T. S. Roland-Jones	did not bat					
O. P. Rayner	did not bat					
S. T. Finn	did not bat					
T. J. Murtagh	did not bat					
Extras	(1 b, 6 lb, 2 nb, 1 w)	10				
Total	(6 wickets, declared, 93.5 overs)	**359**				

Fall of wickets:

1-1 (Robson, 0.6 ov), 2-2 (Compton, 3.6 ov), 3-200 (Gubbins, 68.1 ov), 4-265 (Malan, 86.4 ov), 5-303 (Simpson, 88.4 ov), 6-359 (Franklin, 93.5 ov)

Yorkshire bowling	Overs	Mdns	Runs	Wkts	Wides	No-Balls	Dots	4s	6s
Sidebottom	13	0	36	1	-	-	57		
Brooks	15	5	48	1	-	-	70		
Bresnan	12	3	33	0	-	1	60		
Patterson	14	5	40	0	-	-	67		
Willey	10	3	21	0	-	-	44		
Azeem Rafiq	18	3	46	1	-	-	76		
Lyth	7.5	0	77	1	-	-	25		
Lees	4	0	51	2	1	-	12		

Yorkshire second innings		Runs	Balls	Mins	4s	6s
A Lyth	c Robson b Roland-Jones	13	16	24	2	-
A. Z. Lees	c Gubbins b Murtagh	20	31	42	2	-
D. J. Willey	c Eskinazi b Murtagh	11	21	28	1	-
G. S. Ballance	c Robson b Finn	30	39	47	1	1
T. T. Bresnan	lbw b Roland-Jones	55	48	68	4	2
*A. W. Gale	b Roland-Jones	22	28	41	3	-
+A. J. Hodd	b Roland-Jones	17	19	27	1	-
Azeem Rafiq	c Simpson b Roland-Jones	4	5	12	-	-
S. A. Patterson	b Finn	2	4	6	-	-
J. A. Brooks	not out	0	0	5	-	-
R. J. Sidebottom	b Roland-Jones	0	1	3	-	-
Extras	(4 lb)	4				
Total	(all out, 35.2 overs)	**178**				

Fall of wickets:
1-27 (Lyth, 5.6 ov), 2-39 (Lees, 10.3 ov), 3-48 (Willey, 12.4 ov), 4-98 (Ballance, 22.2 ov), 5-153 (Bresnan, 29.5 ov), 6-160 (Gale, 31.5 ov), 7-174 (Azeem Rafiq, 33.6 ov), 8-178 (Patterson, 34.6 ov), 9-178 (Hodd, 35.1 ov), 10-178 (Sidebottom, 35.2 ov)

Middlesex bowling	Overs	Mdns	Runs	Wkts	Wides	No-Balls	Dots	4s	6s
Murtagh	8	1	28	2	-	-	34		
Roland-Jones	12.2	0	54	6	-	-	40		
Rayner	5	0	32	0	-	-	15		
Finn	10	0	60	2	-	-	24		

Result: Middlesex won by 61 runs

Day One: Middlesex: 208/5 (Gubbins 120*, Franklin 21*; 82 overs)
Day Two: Yorkshire: 235/6 (Bresnan 72*, Azeem Rafiq 20*; 69 overs)
Middlesex Day Three: 81/2 (Gubbins 39*, Malan 37*; 38 overs)

Notes
and Acknowledgements

Nearly a decade ago – in 2009 – I wrote a book called *A Last English Summer*, which was my lame excuse to saunter around the country for six months and do nothing but watch cricket. The book did have a purpose, however. The shape of the game was changing, and I set out to capture things as they were before a tipping-point was reached (nothing but the rapid speed of the change I foresaw has surprised me since).

The same motivation lies behind *The Kings of Summer*. I wanted to preserve one match before the Championship underwent its 2017 upheaval – especially since I suspect that other upheavals will follow (though I am looking forward to watching day-night Championship cricket).

The circumstances surrounding Durham's subsequent relegation quickly justified my decision. That story isn't mentioned in the main text because, apart from my reflections on the past, I have deliberately written about only what had happened *during* the game and my knowledge of it as a spectator. For example, like every other watcher I discovered the day after the match finished that Andrew Gale found James Franklin in the Gents when he went into the Middlesex dressing room to agree on a declaration target. I record it here as a consequence. I also record the size of the crowd, which over four days was over 20,000.

One other point. I refer to the Ridings, aware that their formal abolition occurred decades ago. I use the term because a) I prefer it and b) it's commonly spoken in Yorkshire.

I have to thank, as ever, my indispensable agent Grainne Fox, and Graham Coster – editor and publisher and splendid chap – for his experience and expertise. I'm indebted to East Preston CC for the use of their net last summer.

My perspective of events may differ from your own, but the copious notes for the book were taken from various vantage points as the game progressed. I recorded in 'real time' what I saw and felt and the memories evoked. I did get some strange sideways glances from people who saw me madly scribbling and no doubt questioned my sanity.

For the reader's convenience I refer only to myself, but I did have the company of good friends. I want to thank the aforementioned Graham as well as Will Ellsworth-Jones and Chris Arnot for being there too. Through the unfortunate circumstance of having to work for a living, my wife Mandy was elsewhere. I wish she hadn't been, but five days away from her reminded me that Frank Sinatra was spot on when he sang of how it's nice to go travelling, but so much nicer to come home.